The 13 Unsung Heroes

The Untold Story

Told by Rudy Molina

Written by Adrian Miguel Nunez

© 2019 By Adrian Miguel Nunez (USMC)

CONTENTS

INTRODUCTION

Chapter 1: Deep in the heart of Texas

Chapter 2: Molina Family Tree

Chapter 3: Product of Pecos

Chapter 4: Walking on Eggshells

Chapter 5: Mexican Manhood

Chapter 6: A Game of Dominoes

Chapter 7: Mother Green and Her Killing Machine

Chapter 8: Bright Yellow Footprints

Chapter 9: Oh Three Forever

Chapter 10: Thirty Days of Lollygagging

Chapter 11: HOLY SH**, VIETNAM

Chapter 12: INCOMING

Chapter 13: The Hut Incident

Chapter 14: My Friend Steve

Chapter 15: National Satan's Day

Chapter 16: Thee Honorable Thirteen

Chapter 17: Short Timer Status

Chapter 18: DEROS

Chapter 19: Survivor's Guilt

CONTENTS

Chapter 20: Uncle Sam's Disciple

Chapter 21: First Class Ticket to Nowhere

Chapter 22: Altar Bound

Chapter 23: My Bundles of Joy

Chapter 24: Hanoi Hannah's Nightmare

Chapter 25: Jolly Green Giant

Chapter 26: SNAGGED

Chapter 27: Buried Alive

Chapter 28: Two Dimes Later

Chapter 29: Free at Last

Chapter 30: The Tenderloin

Chapter 31: Out of Bounds

Chapter 32: Damage Control

Chapter 33: Oak Ridge Horizons

(Bonus Chapter) Calling All Battalion Scouts

Acknowledgements

Echoes of an Angel

About the Author

INTRODUCTION

As I sit here writing my life story, I realize one important fact. Life is as good as it gets nowadays. At least that's the view from my eyes. I stare at my fireplace that is burning with worthy size logs. The logs crackle and I still snap my head when I hear that popping noise. The PTSD (Post Traumatic Stress Disorder) still spooks me. The flames change colors as the fire burns on. The hottest of the fire is almost a gleaming white. The cooler pieces break off and fall to the fireplace floor. They are orange and red colored. Sitting here watching my fireplace going in full effect, it's almost like watching my life flash before my eyes. Some memories have gone up in smoke, some have been burning in my soul forever. Those awful ones are the worst. I wish they could be ripped out of my heart for good. They just never leave me. They just keep on burning. I deal with it head on and live day to day. I can't out run it or hide from it even if I tried.

I live a peaceful life secluded in a small mining town named Coulterville. It's in Central California thirty miles west of Yosemite National Park. I live with my wife Beatriz along with our animals we care for. Nestled away from all the hustle and bustle of city life. Just the way I like it. I can tell you one thing though: it wasn't always that way. I have lived in many states and many cities throughout the United States. Some by choice, some by force. We'll get to that later.

I grew up in an extremely abusive home in Pecos, Texas. I have one brother and six sisters. As it was the norm to have big families back in those days, contraceptives weren't very popular back then. Neither were televisions. After living in Texas my entire childhood, I never could imagine how my life would forever be changed. The year was 1967 when I joined the United States Marine Corps. Once I stepped on those yellow footprints at the Marine Corps Recruit Depot San Diego (MCRD), I had no idea what was in store for me. None whatsoever.

It is my time in the Marine Corps that is the sole purpose of writing this story. In October 1967, I was shipped to a small, tropical country 10,000 miles away from home. The country's name was Vietnam. Located in Southeast Asia. The Vietnam War was kicking off to an ultimate high. I was stationed in Vietnam during some of the worst battles. The TET offensive which included Khe Sanh, Hue, and my very worst: The Battle of My Loc. Its small village that sits off the Northern edge of the Cua Viet River. So close to the DMZ (demilitarized zone) that separated North and South Vietnam. North Vietnam stood for communism while the South was anti-communism. Screw the politics, we were immersed in heavy fighting in Vietnam. There have been many firefights and many dates I can't remember.

January 20th 1968 is the day I will never forget. It's the day that the Battle of My Loc occurred. The heroism I witnessed that day was unbelievable. It was also the day thirteen Marine brothers fell that day. They died side by side fighting for each other. Medals that were posthumously awarded ranged from The Bronze Star all the way to the Navy Cross. The conspicuous acts of valor displayed that day and beyond are to be told to the world. Told the RIGHT way.

There's been "disputed accounts" surrounding the actual events that took place that fateful day in January. These "accounts" have been told in a book written by Ron Kovic. He was my former squad leader in Vietnam. We were part of an elite 10-man Scout Team. We were called Battalion Scouts. H&S Co, 1st AMTRAC battalion, 3rd Marine Division. Kovic's high-strung medal hound mentality led us into those open sand dunes that day. We NEVER should've been exposed out in the open the way we did. The 803rd North Vietnamese Army Regiment were waiting for us that day. Dug in deep and heavily armed.

His book tells inaccurate events that never took place. He was NEVER left out alone in the open. I know this fact because I NEVER left him. He wasn't left out alone to die. Trust me, I had all my senses and was not wounded. He was. NO Marine retreats from a battle. In fact, we run TOWARDS the fight. I'm writing this story to bestow honor to those thirteen Marines who paid the ultimate price that day. They deserve all the honor. One of those Marines happened to be my best friend. His name was Steve Sandor Sarossy. He was from Fairview, Ohio. He along the other twelve Marine brothers are located on the Vietnam Wall on Panel 34. They are also honored in MCRD Parris Island. A stain glass window commissioned by my Executive Officer Major Throm is displayed there inside the base chapel. It includes all their names.

The Battle of My Loc will be told accurately here and can be proven as such. I wish that I could delete that day forever. January 20th, 1968 is a date that's branded onto my soul. 51 years later, it seems like yesterday. I know it will always stay with me till my dying day. It never goes away nor does the pain of losing my friend Steve. The valor, courage, and bravery must be told. Told to the world in a THUNDEROUS voice. They must be honored as they fell: Heroes who sacrificed their own lives to save others.

My life after Vietnam was a spiral of twists and turns. I had trouble with my relationships and didn't live up to my potential in the coming years. I went to Vietnam for a second tour and came back even more disgruntled, more lost. I suffered from PTSD and never was the same. The only waves of joy that has ever been in my life are my three daughters. Their names are Gisela, Zenia, and Lynn. My three beautiful angels sent to me from God himself. I'm so grateful for them being in my life even after so many failures on my part, so much time lost due to my poor decision making.

I'll also talk about my career in the U.S. Border Patrol/ INS (Immigration Naturalization Service). My ultimate downfall due to my choices I made. This led to my incarceration that sent me off to Federal Prison for over two decades. I lost it all. My job, my benefits, my wife, and time away from my children. Just like that. During those twenty-two years in prison I wasn't called Rodolfo Molina Jr anymore. I was Federal Inmate # 31810-008. I have nothing to hide. I will talk in detail about my years in those concrete jungles of hell. When I walked out of federal custody in 2012, I gave the prison one last look and flipped it the bird. I knew I'd never return to a life of incarceration EVER. I have kept my promise to myself since then.

Since my release from federal custody, my parents have passed away. I have done my best to restore my relationships with my girls. I've remarried and live a simple, peaceful life. I enjoy hunting, fishing, and anything that requires being outdoors.

Time has changed, towns have changed, and people have changed. One thing that has NEVER changed is my goal to tell the story of these thirteen Marines. I have thought of my fallen Marine brothers every single day. Whether I was a civilian or prisoner, I woke up to that very memory. My main goal has always been to tell their story the way it ACTUALLY happened. The way I saw it from my eyes.

No matter how old you get you should ALWAYS live life to the fullest. As you get older you appreciate everyday even more. At least I do. Reality is we all die someday. I want to tell this story before I turn into Mr. Magoo. Nobody can out run Father Time. I'm 71 now and probably have a solid ten years left on earth. I'm hoping for more. With the time the Lord has blessed me on earth, I have no right to bitch or complain. Each day on earth is a blessing and should be treated as such. For those who are no longer on earth anymore, they'd given anything for just one more day. That I can assure you of. Why I survived Vietnam, I have no idea. I've felt so guilty for many years. Wondering why I survived and they didn't. At certain points of my life, it's almost driven me to suicide. NOW is the time to honor these thirteen heroes. Its ALL for them............The 13 Unsung Heroes.

"When you throw dirt, you lose ground"

-Texan Proverb-

CHAPTER 1: DEEP IN THE HEART OF TEXAS

Romeo Umbrella Delta Yankee......that's my name in the phonetic alphabet. RUDY. My full name is Rodolfo Molina Jr. I was born to Rodolfo Molina Sr. and Genoveva Martinez Molina on April 26th, 1947. I was born in a booming town in southern Texas named Laredo. A lot of my ancestors were born and raised there as well. I guess the Molina roots started there decades ago.

I was the third born out of eight siblings. My only brother Richard and I were always tight. I had six sisters as well. The Molina children went in this order: Mary, Sylvia, Me, Trine, Richard, Hilda, Gloria, and Velma was the youngest. Throughout our years of childhood, my brother Richard and I were bestowed the family "workhorses" if I may. I'll get to that more in a few.........

My Dad was always working on the farms according to my Mother Genoveva. She was a woman of such love, such undisturbed peace, nothing poisonous in her soul. She loved us and I always felt special around her. Most people know that Texas is a land rich of oil and crops. My Dad was a foreman for a group of men called "Braceros." Let me explain.

A "bracero" in Spanish means a man who uses his arms and hands. Hence a ranch hand in a nutshell. These "braceros" were from Mexico and would be recruited by Farm Placement Services. They would usually be paid lower pay and horrible work hours. Labor laws DID NOT APPLY TO THEM. TRUST ME.

These braceros were allowed by the federal government to come into the United States for a season of harvest depending on the local farmers needs.

Braceros were recruited ONLY if domestic labor could not be found in the United States. This was always a shortage and Americans rarely took jobs doing "stoop labor." No matter what pay was offered, the braceros would get the work. Farmers' would continuously go to the Farm Placement Services season after season. The agencies would recruit via radio and newspapers. Both in the United States AND across the border. They'd basically "order" a number of braceros for their harvest three months out. When the harvest was a week out, the farmer would re-visit the agency to make sure his braceros were going to be in town on time. The main crop picked in Texas was cotton. By hand too.

They usually lived in a farmhouse, outdoor barn, or shacks. They came to the United States with the clothes on their backs and a sack full of dreams. If the Farmers didn't get enough help when the crops were ready for harvest, their profits went spinning down the toilet. It's that simple. On that same note, most braceros were manhandled and treated like dog shit. Their screams had no voice no matter how loud they could shout. If they pissed or moaned, they were sent back to Mexico. They'd be placed on "black ball lists "where they'd never be hired in the U.S. again.

In 1947, my Dad's company moved 430 miles northwest to a town in the Texas panhandle. The town's name was Pecos. We ended up moving there. A brand, new beginning for the Molina family. The majority of my childhood would be spent in Pecos. My brother Richard still lives there today.

"The most important thing in the world is family and love"

-John Wooden-

CHAPTER 2: MOLINA FAMILY TREE

My family roots were spun in Laredo in its own little historic web. At least that's the way I see it. My grandparents from my Dad's side were Gregorio Molina and Juana Mendiola. They were both born in Laredo, Texas. My great grandparents were Antonio Molina and Juana Zapata de Molina. He was from Laredo Texas and she was from Mexico.

This gets interesting on my great grandfather Antonio. He was a soldier that fought for the Confederacy during the Civil War days. His commanding officer was General Benavides and served under the 33rd Regiment, India Company. A lot of Americans fail to realize one key point. This point was many Mexican nationals and or Mexican Americans fought for the Confederacy. They have documents and muster lists naming all soldiers.

My great grandmother Juana Zapata de Molina was said to be the cousin of Emiliano Zapata. He was a Mexican General who joined forces with General Pancho Villa. Villa was by far the biggest Mexican revolutionist at the time. He opposed all U.S. forces and Mexican opposition. His luck finally ran out in 1923 when he was assassinated in a small town called Parral. He was hit nine times killing him instantly.

On my Mom's side, my grandparents were Indalesio Martinez and Trinedad Martinez. They too were born in Laredo Texas. My sister Trine was named after my grandmother. My great grandfather was Indalesio Dias. He was reportedly a soldier who fought directly under General Villa's army. Many battles and many years of loyalty together.

It's pretty interesting to see what warriors we had in our family. The stories have been told over the years with paperwork to hold validity. Underneath each battle, each family, there are many dark secrets. Some are shameful and embarrassing but they must be told. It's the only way to find atonement, to breathe peace.

"Texas is a blend of valor and swagger"

-Carl Sandburg-

CHAPTER 3: PRODUCT OF PECOS

Our first house we lived in was 15 miles outside of Pecos on a large farm. Dad's boss Bob Ferguson owned the house and land. Next door in the back was a large barn. There were fields upon fields of cotton. It seemed never ending to be honest. Richard and I went inside the barn one day to snoop around. Inside we found a world of dismay. Around forty Army style cots lined the whole barn floor. Blankets folded neatly laid perfect on the edge of each cot. Homemade clotheslines were hung at different ends of the pillars. Shirts, pants, socks, and drawers dried on each line. A few milk crates were used as a makeshift table. This was the home of the braceros working our fields. Dad was their foreman and they all loved working for him. It as a little city within.

I attended Earl Bell Elementary School in Pecos. My siblings and I used to wait for the school bus to pick us up on the main highway road. Mom would always be the one to walk us all out to the main highway. My Dad never participated in things like that with us. He'd be in the field working by 5am. His world was work, women, and booze. The road to our house was a ¼ mile in. She'd stand there with us until the bus came. Once it came, we loaded up for our daily voyage to school. We'd wave to Mom as far as we could see her. She wouldn't move until we were out of her sight. What a woman.

Around the age of nine years old, we were hit by a devastating act of God. Texas is in the path of what people call "tornado alley." Especially in the Texas panhandle where Pecos is located. Oklahoma really gets the worst of it in my opinion. A twister came ripping down the highway and turned directly to our house. My Mom grabbed all of us kids tight. We huddled in a small circle near the door jam in the closet. I distinctively recall my Mom showing zero fear. The twister roared through the house shredding the roof to bits. Once it passed my heart was still pumping with adrenaline. Seeing my Mom calm in that moment didn't do me no good. I hated twisters.

Next thing you know my Dad comes inside the shredded house with the braceros following. Here we are all huddled up and they were outside working the fields. That's some hardcore stuff there. He showed little emotion towards us. He looked more pissed that the roof and pieces of the walls were missing. I thought to myself "now what are we going to do? "

We ended up moving in the actual town of Pecos. My Dad had to rent a house now. This house was a turd pile compared to Mr. Ferguson's farm house. No running water, no toilet inside the house. We had an outhouse in the backyard away from the house. Ain't that a bitch. If there was a hailstorm outside and you needed to use the bathroom, you were screwed. It was outdoors or hold it. Miserable times I tell you.

To add to the misery, we were forced to sleep on the cold floor. Now my Dad was a foreman as I stated earlier. He was in charge of around forty braceros. He made really good money. The problem was he had developed a few nasty habits. Women and drinking heavily in the town bars. His weekly paycheck found its way towards those vices regularly.

This made me build a lot of anger towards my Dad. Here he was drinking and blowing his paycheck while we're barely getting by. To top that off, he began to become VERY abusive to all of us. When he came home wasted (which was almost daily), your ass puckered when you heard that wooden door screech open. He obviously didn't know what "noise control" meant as he would crash through the house bumping into furniture. I began to hate my Father. I don't really know if I am ashamed to say that now, but it's the way I felt back then. When I looked into his eyes, I let him know I couldn't stand him. He could read it too. He just chose to ignore our feelings. I can assure you my Mom and siblings felt EXACTLY the same.

"Smile in the mirror. Do that every morning and you'll start to see a big difference in your life"

-Yoko Ono-

CHAPTER 4: WALKING ON EGGSHELLS

The Dad's drinking and the abuse we endured were unbearable. Hell, I didn't even want to come home from school anymore. To make matters worse, my Dad started to pull me straight from the bus to the fields. I started driving the tractor on the fields after a few minutes of instructions being yelled at me. My Dad treated his braceros better than he treated me. That's just the facts.

I started watching patterns occur on the weekends. The braceros along with my Dad would go into town to the local bars. I had made myself a shine box and would hang outside the bars offering shines to the braceros. I charged 25 cents a shine and made myself a pocket full of coins. It was easy money and I shined fast. I'd laugh in my head as I heard the men talking amongst themselves. Their stories ranged from if they were going to get laid to their families they had back in Mexico.

I'd take my earnings and go to the candy store with my neighborhood friends. One of my friends was named Eutimio Ramirez. He was a cool cat and we'd hang out in the alley. We'd make a fire in the back with rocks containing our little flame. Sitting there talking about our lifestyles, Texas, and who was the cutest girl at school. School, fields, and sleep was my routine now. When I had downtime, believe me I took full advantage of that.

Another good friend I had in Pecos was Max Hernandez. His nickname was "El Prieto." He was called that due to his dark skin color. I would be in awe due to his unusual ways. One in particular had everyone talking in town. This was his habit of NEVER wearing shoes. When I say never, I mean NEVER. If a snowstorm hit, he'd walk around the streets unconcerned. You wouldn't see him wincing in pain or falling. He acted like he had a pair of combat boots on. The bottoms of his feet were atrocious. Totally littered with callouses.

Things started changing once again. Life is like a spinning curveball that never lands in the catcher's mitt. We moved into a new house in Pecos. The address was 1202 E. 6th Street. Once again, Dad's boss Bob Ferguson paid for it in cash. Dad made the monthly payments to him. It had running water and one toilet but hey it was INSIDE the house. Enough said. You could've sworn we hit the jackpot. No more out house at 3am to go take a piss.

During the coming months we came home and my Mom had a smile on her face. On the small entertainment set sat a brand, new television set. We couldn't believe our eyes. We turned it on and started watching all of the sitcoms playing. The Andy Griffith Show, Leave it to Beaver, Lassie, etc. This was the best thing since sliced bread. We were envied by all of the other households on the block. Nobody had a television set except for us. You would hear our friends and neighbors saying things like "The Molina family are the richest on the block. "I used to get a kick out of that kind of buffoonery.

I figured out another hustle that I could make some serious coin. I had all my friends pestering me daily now. They all wanted to come over to watch TV. I started charging each of my friends a nickel to come inside. Hell, by the end of the week every neighborhood kid was in our house. My Dad was out in the fields working all the time. My Mom never complained about the constant flow of company. She thought I was just being nice. I was nice to any kid who had a nickel to spare. Otherwise you didn't enter my house. Just like the movies. NO NICKEL, NO TICKET. They were just as addicted as I was. What a racket I had going on. Always turning a profit. My folks never discovered this.

One thing that kept up the horror at the Molina household was the abuse. Dad still drank heavily and would come in smelling like hookers' perfume. The more and more I witnessed, the more hatred brewed towards him. My Mom would sometimes send me and Richard to live with our Aunt Cipriana. She lived back in Laredo. She'd take us in and we'd have to start fresh there. New schools, new friends, new everything. What a pain in the ass.

When we FINALLY started getting comfortable to our new surroundings, Mom would send for us. ARE YOU KIDDING ME? We just were getting acclimated to Laredo and now we get yanked out AGAIN. Man, we hated this with a passion. It really screwed up my brother and I. When you're a kid though, you don't call your own shots. Plain and simple. This monkey business went on for years and it just sucked more and more. I think my Mom sent us away so we wouldn't have to deal with my abusive Dad. She took the blunt of the abuse. I could only imagine the gazillion tears she swallowed in order to see us smile. It's tough to even think about. We were blessed to have her as our Mother. Wish I could tell her that one more time.

"Macho and muscle have nothing to do with being a real man"

-Anonymous-

CHAPTER 5: MEXICAN MANHOOD

Around the age of 11, my Dad told my Mom we needed to be working in the fields full time. This meant after school it was straight to the fields till the sun fell. Homework, do it later. Dinner, don't ask. Sleep, you can sleep when you're dead. Those were the typical answers we got from our Warden (aka Dad). I'm serious when I say we were basically full-time braceros. The only thing I hated more than ever is he kept our pay. I knew it wasn't going to the household bills. It was going into his personal "slush fund." This would pay for his whores and his booze. What a worm.

As if the abuse and my career in the fields weren't enough, my Dad gets this bright idea. He said my Uncle Juan and Aunt Salome wanted us to go to Michigan with them. They lived in Laredo at the time. Coming from my Dad, I knew this wouldn't be good. Mary, Sylvia, and I were sent down via the bus to Laredo. As soon as we arrived, we discovered our summer future. We'd be heading to Michigan to pick cherries and strawberries. YOU GOT TO BE KIDDING ME. I KNEW THIS WAS GOING TO BE A TRIP FROM HELL.

With my Aunt and Uncle inside the truck driving, they packed us along with our other cousins, in the bed of this huge truck. Almost like a deuce and a half Army truck. Just not that big. No cover just open bed period. If it happened to be cold or rain on the way, OH WELL. Three days of pure misery just getting to Michigan. When we arrived, I was tired. We all were. The very NEXT day it was out in the fields doing "stoop labor." We were picking cherries and strawberries from sun up to sundown. This slave labor lasted the entire summer. When it was finally over, we asked my Aunt Salome how much money we earned. She told us that our earnings went towards living expenses such as food, gas, water, shelter, etc. I just about soiled myself in stupidity. NO MONEY? What the hell were we out there for then? They made a lot of dough off our backs. I'm SURE of that. Its not like they were feeding us lobster tails and beluga every night. We ate bare minimum and slept on cots for Pete's sake.

When we got back our jobs around the fields kept increasing. More responsibilities same pay pretty much. Richard and I were allowed to keep our pay during our high school years finally. We helped pay bills but we also got to have our fair share. This was going great especially when we started "flagging."

This job paid great. Richard and I got it down to a science. Flagging is when two people take 15 steps in the opposite direction. Then you have a "lane" for the crop duster to know where to spray the pesticides on. Once a pass occurs, you move 15 steps in the same direction. This makes sure the crop duster overlaps and don't miss any of the crops. If you underestimate the width, a crop-dusting plane could possibly take your head off. These are the dangers of it. We'd be choking on those pesticides during the whole process. They now call it "aerial application." It'll always be known to me as crop dusting.

If we were in a Union, my Dad's operation would've been shut down. So hazardous, so dangerous. But we loved it. This was pretty much how our lives were spent during junior high and my high school years. School, work, sleep. No sports, no extracurricular activities. I was able to save up some money. In high school, I started dating this beautiful Mexican girl. Her name was Jessie. She was such a doll and I was crazy for her. I felt so much pride that I was her boyfriend. The funny part was we never had sex. I tried to many times but she said she wasn't that kind of girl.

I bought myself a 57' Chevy with a 327 engine. Damn that car had some muscle. I had a badass car, and a smoking hot girlfriend. Something was missing though. I knew I wasn't going to stay at home forever. Once I could leave, I'd be gone. Dad's abusive and pompous ways never jived with me. Maybe that's why I've never been a hard-core drinker. I never wanted to be the type of prick he was when he drank. I used to drink socially. I haven't had a drink in over thirty years. No need to.

I kept hearing about this country on the news. I couldn't even pronounce it correctly but finally did: Vietnam. It was in Southeast Asia and the talk of oncoming conflict in that country became the nightly news. In 1961, John F. Kennedy that the United States would send more advisers and support to the South Vietnamese. This was the first time I heard anyone speak about "the domino theory."

"The theory of Communism may be summed up in one sentence: Abolish all private property"

-Karl Marx-

CHAPTER 6: A GAME OF DOMINOES

Back in the 1950's, the Cold War between the United States and the Soviet Union (present day Russia) was at its peak. Both countries fought for strategic alliances with others. The United States was for democracy while the Soviet Union was for Communism. In April of 1954, President Dwight D "Ike" Eisenhower spoke during a national conference. He mentioned the "domino theory" for the first time.

The domino theory was considered a reasonable threat. The French were getting annihilated in Vietnam. In 1954, the country ended up splitting into North and South Vietnam. This was the beginning of the French withdrawal from Vietnam permanently. The North was for communism while the South was all for democracy via U.S. aid. The DMZ (DEMILITARIZED ZONE) divided the country in half. It was also littered with thousands of land mines by both sides.

From the mid 1950's to 1963, The United States send over U.S. advisers to combat communist movements. Intense fighting ensued. The support went from advisers to arms and supplies. It only grew as each year passed. By the time John F. Kennedy was elected President of the United States in 1960, we were knee deep in VIETNAM. Aid wise I mean. Financially most though. The terrain shown on television were thick, canopy jungles to mountain ranges. Very high altitude. Tropical weather that included a wet monsoon season.

By 1963, my brother and I were hot shot flaggers. At least we thought so. We were earning a decent wage and discovering new freedoms by the day. I'd be hanging out with my girlfriend on the weekends or my pals Eutimio and Max. Max was always a hit and miss though. He was basically the terror of the town. Always into illegal activity committing crimes. He went to the juvenile boys' ranch which was a lock up camp for boys under 18. He went there too many times to count. It's probably the only time he wore shoes too. After years of him pestering law enforcement in Pecos, they were fed up. They gave Max two options. GET THE HELL OUT OF PECOS FOREVER OR PRISON FOR LIFE.

One day the Sheriff drove Max out to the county line. According to him, the Sheriff pointed West and told him "California's that way." Max walked to California. Yes, WALKED. He finally arrived in Merced, CA three months later. I currently reside an hour away from him. We still talk on the phone and I visit him every so often. I always look at his feet and think "damn that guy put some miles on those things." It's almost biblical, LOL.

Tragedy struck the Molina family real hard that year. My older Sylvia had become pregnant. It was her first born and she had been really excited. When she gave birth to her son Amado aka "Amadito" as we called him, she died unexpectedly. I don't remember the exact details on that nor do I care to. All I remember is my Mother was crushed. As usual, I never saw an emotion come out of my Dad. Sad to say, Amadito met his demise way too early as well. When he was forty-two, he was killed in an automobile accident. It goes to show how precious each and everyday we have on earth is. We all loved our nephew very much.

In November of 1963, South Vietnamese President Ngo Dinh Diem was assassinated. It was part of a military coup. He'd fell out of favor with the U.S. in the last years of his term. The U.S. still supported the South Vietnamese with money, arms, advisers, and supplies. Some speculate the Central Intelligence Agency (CIA) had some part in Diem's demise. I wouldn't doubt that since they were in Vietnam "advising." Three weeks later, that same agency would gain worldwide attention.

On November 22nd, 1963, President John F. Kennedy rode in a motorcade with Texas Governor John Connally and their wives. They were in Dallas, Texas. President Kennedy had traveled there to smooth over some friction. The rift was between the Democratic party and conservative Governor John Connally. They were driven in a 1961 Lincoln Continental four door convertible limousine. It would be the last time any U.S. President was allowed such luxury.

At 12:30 pm (central time) as the Presidential limo rode through Dealey Plaza, gunshots rang out. When the smoke cleared, President Kennedy was mortally wounded. The "kill shots" were one through the neck. The other struck his head. He died in a Parkland Texas hospital an hour later. Vice President Lyndon B Johnson was quickly sworn in as the 36th U.S. President a short time later. It was aboard Air Force One. His nickname was LBJ. His wife's name was Lady Bird. Governor Connally was wounded in the back and suffered a collapsed lung. He recovered from his wound. It was later discovered both had been struck by a high-powered Italian bolt action rifle. Although Lee Harvey Oswald was deemed the alleged assassin, the CIA was highly speculated to be behind President Kennedy's death. Many believed Oswald was simply a "patsy." Another word for a "scapegoat." He ended up meeting his violent demise a few days later. Dallas nightclub owner Jack Ruby shot Oswald while being escorted by Texas constables. All caught on television. Live by the gun, die by the gun. LBJ, now President and Texas native himself, would place the United States full-fledged into Vietnam. It would not only be an advisory role. The U.S. would be in a WAR. By 1965, it was officially called the Vietnam War.

"Not all those who wonder are lost"

-J.R.R. Tolkien-

CHAPTER 7: MOTHER GREEN AND HER KILLING MACHINE

Around 1965, I was still working in the fields with my Dad. I quit high school after my junior year. I was bored with school and had zero intentions of going to college. Although life in Pecos sometimes seemed redundant, one memory clearly sticks out. My brother Richard joined a band in Pecos. They were called "Mondie and the Mystics." They were amazing. Richard jammed on his saxophone like nobody else. Man, they played some EXTRAORDINARY music. I'm not just saying that cause he's my brother, but they were THEE BEST in my eyes.

Everywhere they'd play, the crowds would follow including me. They played the best "Tex-Mex" music I've ever heard of. School events, dance halls, town festivals, weekend garage parties, etc. You name it they played it. It was a wonderful feeling being around the band. I felt an abundance of pride knowing my little brother could jam on the sax the way he did. I couldn't play an instrument if my life depended on it. I was content listening and dancing to the Mystics' music. Believe it or not, I still play the music today: in my head and on my phone. It never left my soul.

I'd been watching John Wayne movies like Sands of Iwo Jima and Operation Pacific since I was a kid. I'd always been impressed by the way the U.S. Marine Corps had been portrayed. The best of the best, the elite. They had the longest boot camp (13 weeks) and the best uniforms (dress blues) in my opinion. You had to be one badass to be a United States Marine. I'd sometimes pass the local recruiting station in Pecos. I was at the end of my rope doing field work. I didn't want to live and die in Pecos forever. I wanted to travel and broaden my horizons.

Months and months went by with very little excitement. I started to see friends joining Vietnam. Some of them came back in flag-draped coffins. I felt a sense to serve my country after witnessing this. I also felt guilty of being here while my friends fought in the Vietnam War. I had made up my mind. I was going to be a United States Marine.

I was going to volunteer and ask for combat duty in Vietnam. That was it end of story. Nobody was going to change my mind. I went to my Mother and asked if I could talk to her. She sat with me on the couch and I told her I was joining the Marine Corps. I explained to her as soon as our conversation was over, I was going to drive to the recruiting station. She just gave me a half smile, half concerned look, and said "ok son."

I could see in her eyes she was happy for me. Happy I was going to leave the abuse my Dad so happily dished out. I bet she'd have left his ass long ago if she didn't have us. Although I felt some guilt, I had to push that aside and move forward. She was chained to that house, that life. I wasn't. I would be happily leaving that life at the doorsteps of 1202 E. 6th Street. I hugged my Mother and left the house. As I peeled away in my 57' Chevy, I saw my Mother outside waiving at me. I waived back excitingly. She was smiling I could see. Although it was heavily overcast in Pecos that March afternoon, her smile illuminated the sky. It was her Godsent love that oozed out of her heart. Her love could light up the darkest caves known to mankind. I miss that even today. That love of hers, that genuine love.

I walked inside the U.S. Marine recruiting station in Pecos. A tall, physically fit Sergeant in blue dress pants and a khaki shirt shook my hand. His name was Sergeant Bosack. We sat down and started to talk about my future with the Marine Corps. I couldn't stop gazing at those immaculate cross rifles below his stripes. The creases on his trousers and blouse were impeccable. I was mesmerized. I couldn't wait to own that uniform, that title: UNITED STATES MARINE. He spoke with confidence and his tone was deep. After doing some initial tests, I passed with flying colors. Sergeant Bosack took my height and weight which was fine. We made an appointment for MEPS (Military Entry Processing Station) and shook hands.

A few days later, I was picked up by Sergeant Bosack and a few other boys. We went to MEPS and we spent all day there. ASVAB test was to see how smart or dumb you were. I scored fairly well but choose my MOS (military occupational specialty). Oh Three Eleven (0311). That was the code for Rifleman; aka GRUNT. The Infantry.

After vaccinations, more paperwork, medical exams, and more waiting, we were called into a large room. All the boys and girls joining the different branches of the Armed Services would be sworn in together. Including me. After we were sworn in, they let us out and we took a break. The recruiters would now be arriving to pick up their respective "poolees" as we were called. Sgt. Bosack asked me "Molina what MOS did you choose?" I responded "OH THREE ELEVEN, SERGEANT." He got super excited. As we got on the highway he said "you'll be kicking ass with mother green and her killing machine. You'll definitely see action on the frontlines Molina. More than you think." He lit a cigarette and smiled. He was blasting the radio loud now. His words would become BEYOND true!

Once we drove up to my house on E. 6th Street, I was excited. Sergeant Bosack turned down the music and we talked briefly. He told me "Molina go get your shit squared away. I'll pick you up in two weeks. Go get laid, see your friends, eat junk food while you can. Cause in two weeks, all the fun shit will be a memory. Carry on." I responded "Yes Sergeant." As I exited the van, I turned to Sgt Bosack and asked" where am I going to go to boot camp?" He laughed and said "MCRD SAN DIEGO." This stood for Marine Corps Recruit Depot, San Diego California.

"Ohhhhhhhhhhh damn, what the hell did I get myself into?"

-Anonymous Recruit-

CHAPTER 8: BRIGHT YELLOW FOOTPRINTS

March 19th 1967 came with excitement. I woke up at 4am knowing this would be my last day here. Last day in Pecos, last day of dealing with my Dad's tormenting ways. I couldn't wait to get the hell out of there. My recruiter Sgt Bosack was set to pick me up at 6am SHARP. My Mother was already up and making me a power breakfast. Bacon, three eggs, and hashed browns. She was excited for me and I could genuinely feel that from her. I'd said goodbye to my other siblings the night before. My Dad walked in to grab his coffee. He gave me a half ass hug and said "good luck Rudy." Off to the fields he went.

Mom and I continued our conversation during breakfast. Around 5:55 am, I heard Sgt Bosack's van pull up to the driveway. I kissed and hugged my Mom goodbye. I grabbed my bag and bolted out the door. My new beginning was about to begin. I was beyond thrilled. I jumped in the van and greeted Sgt Bosack. He said "LET'S ROLL RUDY." Sgt Bosack burned rubber as we sped away on our three-hour journey. Headed to El Paso International Airport for my outgoing flight to San Diego, California.

On the entire flight I was super pumped. I knew the Marine Corps boot camp was the toughest. I knew I'd do well and imagined what the "depot" looked like. That's what Marines called MCRD. As we landed in San Diego, I gazed out the plane window. I could see these huge sprawling buildings to my right. They were all an ugly, mustard color. A huge sign was posted on the depot facing the airport. It said "JOIN NOW, CALL 1-800 MARINES." There was a huge Eagle, Globe, and Anchor next to it. The logo of the Marine Corps. It's also what you receive once you become a U.S. MARINE. Perfect recruiting tactic in my opinion.

Once off the plane, I headed to the USO in the airport. Around 25 other "poolees" were waiting. I checked in and sat in a chair. Around twenty minutes later, a Marine Corps Drill Instructor (DI) stepped inside. "GRAB YOUR SHIT AND FOLLOW ME GENTLEMEN. QUICKLY, QUICKLY, QUICKLY!" We all followed this DI who wore a round "campaign cover" as they're called. Once outside we were hurried on this white bus. Once we all were loaded up, the bus started moving. The driver was an old, white guy. He had to be in his 60's. He was smoking a foul-smelling cigar. He was smirking at us as we climbed on the bus. At that moment, I wanted to smack that old geezer. I think he knew what laid ahead for us.

We could see the big sign "MARINE CORPS RECRUIT DEPOT, SAN DIEGO, CA "as we entered the gates. The guards at the gates were smiling and pointing to us. I guess they got a kick of seeing busloads of recruits pull in to the awaiting hell. As our bus pulled forward, we drove to what was the "RECEIVING" barracks. There were about six other DI's waiting for us. Other recruits were on these bright yellow footprints. One DI leapt onto the bus. He screamed "GET THE FUCK OFF MY BUS." We were LAUNCHED off the bus with screaming DI's in every direction. One recruit pissed himself. Another fainted on his very footprints he stood on. You think I'm joking but it DOES happen. After our initial induction to MCRD SD, we were hurriedly rushed into the receiving barracks. After haircuts, shakedowns, paperwork, and yelling, we fell asleep a day later. What a miserable two days.

Marine Corps jargon was something you had to get used to. Your hand was now called a dickskinner. Left was port. Right was starboard. The bathroom was a head. A wall was a bulkhead. Your hat was a cover. Your head was a grape. Your bed a rack. Food was chow. Pants were trousers. A shirt a blouse. You get the picture? You had to forgot any civilian words and transform FAST into Marine Corps terminology. If you didn't, off to the "sandpit" you went.

The next five weeks were spent on the depot. Days just flew by as we learned Marine Corps history, cadences, formations, physical training of all sorts, etc. We went through numerous medical and dental checks. Paperwork by the truckload. Man, the first two weeks were hell. You get four DI's that stay with your platoon the whole 13 weeks. One is the Senior Drill Instructor. A lot of hurry up and wait. After that things really took off. You got used to speaking in "third person" lingo. If you wanted to know something you'd have to scream "THIS RECRUIT REQUESTS KNOWLEDGE." If you needed to use the HEAD, you would scream "THIS RECRUIT REQUESTS TO MAKE A HEAD CALL." Once you heard a DI respond "GO", YOU BETTER BE RUNNING TO YOUR DESTINATION.

Every time you'd screw up, you'd get PT'd to death. That's short for physical training. San Diego airport was a stones' throw away from the depot. Sometimes I'd get caught daydreaming while doing marching drills on the parade deck. I'd see these planes taking off and think" those lucky bastards are going somewhere fun. I'm stuck here in this crap." Then I'd get busted by a DI...... Gunny Sgt Diel. "MOLINA GET IN THE FUCKIN SANDPIT YOU MAGGOT." After a few hundred pushups or "dying cockroach" exercises, I'd be told "REEEEECOVER." I'd jump to my feet and haul ass back to formation. A cloud of dirt and Gunny Sgt Diel trailing right behind me. He was the one I remember clearly. That guy hated my guts. I always got stuck with the shittiest details, fire watches, etc. When you're in boot camp, there's always one that'll ride your ass the entire 13 weeks. Mine was Gunny Sgt Diel. A short, bald guy with "small man syndrome" to the tenth power. The shit you remember forever. LOL.

Weeks six through eleven were probably the best time in boot camp. We moved to Range 33 on Camp Pendleton. It was about an hour and a half bus ride from the depot. This is where we would do grass week and "rifle quals." Short for rifle qualifications. Here you would see how much you learned with your beloved M-14 rifle. We would be on the ranges ALL DAY after morning PT and breakfast. Time flew by even faster. The next thing you know, I'd qualified EXPERT in both rifle and pistol. We also fired the M-60 machine gun. They called that the "PIG." It was gas operated and belt fed. What a powerful weapon that was.

Another favorite was the "thump gun." The M-79 grenade launcher fired a 40mm grenade. It was accurate and one shot. When you opened it to reload it made a "blook" sound. Hence the nickname "blooker" as was commonly used by NAM vets. They swore by it as a lifesaver in combat. I'd find out later for myself how true that was.

The last three weeks of boot camp winded down quickly. Final drills, inspections, PT Tests and map reading tests. All completed and all passed. I was in phenomenal shape. I put on my "dress blues" and stared in the mirror. I was ready to graduate. After 13 weeks of backbreaking hell, I'd earned the coveted title "UNITED STATES MARINE." The pride I felt as I graduated that hot, July morning has never left me. If you are a U.S. Marine, I'm sure you can relate. It's a fraternal brotherhood of the highest order. I can't explain that enough.

Once we graduated and handed our EGA's (eagle globe and anchor), we were told to come back to our barracks to receive our orders. After half the platoon was called, I finally got mine. "MOLINA, 0311 INFANTRY." I hightailed it out of there. I had to catch a bus to the airport. I was off to Pecos, Texas for my ten day "boot leave." I had a nice hot meal in the airport as I awaited my flight. Once we were on the plane and airborne, I looked out the window at MCRD SD. I could see recruits down there and laughed. Finally, I was the "bastard" going somewhere fun. I smiled as the plane banked right and now heading to Texas. I drifted into my thoughts for the next two hours.

"The deadliest weapon in the world is a Marine and his rifle"

-Gen. John "Black Jack" Pershing-

CHAPTER 9: Oh Three Forever

After a well deserved 10-day rest, it was back to San Diego. I landed and boarded a military bus to Camp Pendleton. It took us an hour and a half to travel the 40 miles from San Diego to Oceanside. Straight up Interstate 5. Always that California traffic. It's even a hundred times worse today. I would be going to (S.O.I.) which was School of Infantry. This would be a ten-week course learning everything a "grunt" would face in Vietnam. Any (MOS) that started with an "OH THREE" was Infantry. 0311 was a rifleman aka a GRUNT. 0331 was a machine gunner. 0341 was a mortar man aka GROUND POUNDER. Pretty simple. This included firing different weapons, calling in artillery or bombing missions, to map reading. On top of that, plenty of "humping." This is when you march with full rucksack, full combat load. You march for MILES. Yes MILES!

ALL non-infantry Marines must go through basic INFANTRY training. It was 24 days long. After that, these Marines would go to their respective schooling. That could be anywhere in the United States. They were housed across SOI on Basilone Road. It was where the "POGS" as we called them. It stood for Person Other than Grunt. We'd call them "pieces of garbage", "desk jockeys", "non-rates." We'd make sure to infiltrate their barracks during weekend liberty or "libo" as we called it. We'd fight with them and tear up their housing. We were gung-ho grunts in training. We would kick each other's ass just for entertainment.

During the 10 weeks at SOI, we were in the field constantly. This was way more rigorous than boot camp. When we did come back to the barracks, we were still handed "C-Rats" to eat. These were food in tins cans. Even though the chow hall was a hundred meters away, we only ate there during libo. The Instructors told us there wouldn't be no hot chow in Vietnam. We'd better start getting used to it now.

The things I remember the most of SOI was certain areas. First was a huge mountain that SOI faced. It was nicknamed "Mount Motherfucker." It earned it too. The hill was so vertical that you could touch it with your hand as you were humping up it. Unbelievable. Another one was called "A trail of tears." A LONG ASS trail and zigzagged up and down hills. When you're carrying a full combat load, believe me you feel it all.

Calling in artillery was some of the hairiest moments there. One digit off and you'd dump your whole platoon with an abundance of explosives. You'd all be dead. We paid full attention to it and made sure all the radio lingo was mastered. Marines who were Vietnam veterans mainly taught the courses. They told us to learn each and every Marine's job in the field. That was critical to your survival. Map reading was just as crucial. You better know where you're going in pitch black darkness.

They'd set up "mock villages" on Camp Pendleton. They were very useful and exact replicas of Vietnam. The instructors stressed how Vietnam was laced with booby traps of all sorts. We would look for trip wires or anything out of the ordinary. After ten weeks of this detailed training, I was ready. My Platoon Sgt was Staff Sergeant Taylor. When we graduated SOI, one by one we were called in his office. Finally, my turn came up. "LANCE CORPORAL MOLINA, GET IN HERE."

Staff Sgt Taylor handed me my orders. I'd be going to the frontlines to fight in Vietnam. I was granted a 30-day leave before shipping out. I went to San Diego airport and caught a flight home. I was going to make the best out of these 30 days. Hell, they possibly could be my last days of fun on earth. By the afternoon, I was pulling up in a taxi to 1202 E.6th Street. There was my beautiful Mother waiting for me with open arms. She stood smiling in the doorway. My Angel from Heaven.

"Courage is knowing what not to fear"

-Plato-

CHAPTER 10: Thirty Days of Lollygagging

My next thirty days was going to be filled with action, fun, and carefree living. Mom made me the best food I could eat. All of my favorite dishes smelled up the house with an irresistible aroma. My brother Richard was my sidekick. I'd spent time with my sister Mary and Trine. I also made time with the little ones. Gloria, Hilda, and Velma were much younger than we were. Sometimes after dinner, I'd just sit in the backyard and watch my little sisters playing. They probably didn't understand where I was headed to and or if they'd ever see me again. I tried to block that out of my head but it was reality. War is war and it brings the worst out of man period. Vietnam was in fact "the killing fields" if I may. Many young American servicemen were dying. Nobody ever said war was pretty.

I wasn't doing nothing but having the time of my life. I thought to myself "Rudy make the last days count." Boy did I ever. I would hang out a lot with Richard. I got to see Mondie and the Mystics play a few more times at parties they were hired to play at. I would invite my friends to these parties and we all had a great time.

I told my girlfriend Jessie Vasquez that I didn't know if I would return alive from Vietnam. She got really sad and told me "don't say that Rudy. You'll be alright." I was still trying to find my way into the sack with her but she just wouldn't budge. Man, that was frustrating. After the last attempt, I gave up. I told her not to wait for me and I wished her the best.

I started to see other girls in town and they were more than willing. We would go out for drinks, hit up the movies, and find our way to a motel. Ending up in the sack with these girls was amazing. I knew I wouldn't be around for a while and I let them all know that. One girl I really stuck with the most in that month was a girl I'll call "Wendy." She wasn't a beauty queen like Jessie but she got the job done. I was in her bedroom almost every night. Come to think of it, my last night I spent it with her.

Saying goodbye to all my friends and family was quite different this time. Now I wasn't going to training or boot camp; I was going to WAR. 10,000 miles away in a tropical country in Southeast Asia. One I never even heard of till 1960. Friends hugged me longer, girls I dated kissed me longer. My family held on tighter. At least that's the way I felt. I wanted to get the hell out of Pecos already.

Once I kissed and hugged my family goodbye, it was back to El Paso International airport. I couldn't wait to start this long journey to Vietnam. I sat inside the concourse near the window sipping on a cup of coffee. I was enjoying watching the planes come and go. I would see their destination and wonder why they were traveling to their respective destinations. Some said "DETROIT" another plane said "SEATTLE" and so on. I was thinking if the concourse screen would light up and say" RUDY MOLINA, YOU'RE PLANE IS HERE TO TAKE YOUR ASS OFF TO VIETNAM. TIME TO GO FIGHT THIS WAR." I swear I was hallucinating. Soon my boarding call came. Just not in that same sentence. It went more like "Flight 426 now boarding to San Francisco." I was on my way to hell. I was excited, scared, nervous, and proud all at once. One thing I NEVER had nor do I to this day. REGRET.

"Put on the full armor of God, so that you can take your stand against the devil's schemes"

-Ephesians 6:11-

CHAPTER 11: HOLY SH**, VIETNAM

The plane started hauling ass down the El Paso runway. Once in the air, I knew this might be my last time seeing Texas; seeing any part of the U.S. EVER AGAIN. I looked out the window and said a "quiet" goodbye. I think I was mentally checking out period. I was adjusting my frame of mind knowing that my life would see no peace for at least a year.

I landed in San Francisco but never left the airport. I had to change planes immediately. I switched over to a huge PAN-AM airlines plane. The plane was loaded with nothing but Marines. As I passed through the rows heading towards the back, the same faces spelled my inner thoughts. The many faces of uncertainty, what we were headed for, and if this would be the last trip of our lives. I could feel that inside when I looked at these other men. I felt that inside times a hundred!

Our trip was one LONG trip. It just made the thoughts of death much worse. I wanted to be in Vietnam already. Our first stop was Anchorage, Alaska. From there we went to Hawaii. Hawaii to Manila, Philippines. Philippines to Okinawa. We never left the airports in any of those cities including San Francisco. Once in Okinawa, we finally disembarked the plane. The stewardesses watching us exit the plane all had tears in their eyes. Each one was beautiful and wearing skimpy flight attendant uniforms. They knew we were going to war. Some uttered "good luck" or "God Bless You" as we exited. Believe me, I was praying heavy I'd survive this tour.

Once in Okinawa, we were briefed in a huge auditorium on base. We endured multiple vaccinations, classes and instructions on what to expect. We were taught simple words in Vietnamese, the terrain in certain areas, the weather, tons of "booby traps" used, etc. We started to hear the word "CHARLIE" by the class instructor. That's what they called the enemy soldiers. Another frequented name used to mock the enemy was "gooks." This was the most derogatory word for the Vietnamese enemy in my opinion. Others included "dinks", "zips", "slopes", etc. This was all new to us. I had never even met an Asian until I joined the military. Let alone a VIETNAMESE. I was never a bigot and got along with everybody. Once the first round sailed over my head from an enemy AK-47 assault rifle, I wanted to slaughter every one of those bastards. I'm sure the others felt the same exact way. WAR IS A MOTHERFUCKER. It'll bring thee absolute worst of out anybody.

After 10 days in Okinawa it was off to Vietnam: FINALLY. The military plane we were on landed on Da Nang airbase. Once the rear of the plane cranked open, DAMN we were hit with a "wave of fire." It was like a humongous vacuum sucking all the air out of our lungs. The intense humidity is something I'd never experienced. I remember one Vietnam Veteran Marine at Camp Pendleton say "The NAM is the devil's den. It's the hottest place on planet earth." He was right. Now I was in Vietnam. The "NAM" as we called it. There it is.

The airstrip was surrounded by multiple bunkers. Each was manned and equipped with an M-60 machine gun. They were spread out in 100-meter intervals I'd say. The airstrip would sometimes come under heavy mortar and artillery attacks. This is why the airbase was heavily guarded by U.S. personnel. Da

Nang laid south of the city of Hue. I hung out there listening to veterans who had a lot of time "in-country." In country meant "in Vietnam." Three days later I was told to get on the convoy that was headed to the Cua Viet river. I was assigned to CAMP KISTLER which was located at the mouth of the Cua Viet River.

We made the convoy in large trucks. They were called "deuce and a half" trucks and were very durable. The trip went without incident and we reached the city of Dong Ha. It was right off HIGHWAY 1. I stayed there for two days learning about the terrain and enemy tactics. We were about 5 miles away from the DMZ (Demilitarized Zone). This line called the DMZ split the country in half. South was for Democracy and North for Communism. It was HEAVILY lined with landmines planted by BOTH sides. Once there we loaded up onto gunboats. This would be the last leg of my journey to CAMP KISTLER. Finally, no more traveling. Time to start my 365 days of hell.

The Marines at Dong Ha talked to us before we left. The NVA regulars (North Vietnamese Army) and the VC (Viet Cong) both operated along the riverbanks. The NVA were highly trained and motivated. They wore green uniforms and green pith helmets. Also, they wore belts with a red communist star on the buckle. Those were considered a prize if you got one. It also meant you whacked the gook who was wearing it. The VC were farmers by day, killers by night. They wore regular clothing like the villagers. They usually wore conical hats called "Non-La's." A Marine Sergeant yelled to us, "MAKE SURE YOU KEEP YOUR FUCKIN EYES PEELED. THE GOOKS LIKE TO TAKE SHOTS AT OUR BOATS FROM THE TREELINE COVER ON THE BANKS. LOOK FOR ANYONE NOT A VILLAGER. ANYONE ARMED OR SHOOTING AT US, WASTE EM."

We loaded onto the gunboats and headed East on the Cua Viet River towards CAMP KISTLER. The trip was about 3 miles or so. I hoped that we'd have zero enemy fire on our way. I kept my eyes peeled and my M-14 rifle close by. The gunboats were hauling ass down the river and we kept our guard up. Sure enough, about five minutes later I saw three Viet Cong soldiers running in the tree line. They started firing at our boat and we returned fire. The distinct "BLAAAP BLAAAP BLAAAP" sounds of their AK-47's were earth shattering. The smell of gunpowder and the crack of our M-14's followed immediately. The enemy rounds riddled the river and sailed right past our heads. The sadistic "death shrieks" of those rounds made my ass pucker tight. PURE TERROR, PURE FEAR. I'm not ashamed to admit it either. A few rounds made a weird impacting sound when striking the boat. It sounded like a rock hitting an empty coke can. It came with a much louder "SNAPPING" sound. It sent chills down my spine. FUCK, THIS IS WAR.

As I was reloading my M-14, I CLEARLY remember seeing one VC running up to the riverbank. He suddenly knelt down on one knee and raised his rifle. I was about to unload on him. The boat gunner opened up on his position before I did. DIRECT HIT. I could see through my iron sights the volley of rounds smashing into the VC's body. His Non-La flew off and his body spun FULL 360. The impacting rounds convulsed his body and he finally landed on the sand. Alive one minute and dead the next. That's how fast you could lose in war. My hands were trembling and this crude thought went whizzing across my mind: RUDY YOU HAVE A LONG WAY TO GO. GET USED TO THIS. YOU'RE IN THE "SHIT" NOW. I looked at the boat gunner. He had a huge grin on his face as he screamed "KIA." That meant "Killed in Action." As we pulled up to the mouth of the Cua Viet River, the boat turned into CAMP KISTLER. Finally, I had reached my destination. WHAT A RUSH!

"Blessed be the Lord my strength which teacheth my hands to war and my fingers to fight"

-Psalm 144:1-

CHAPTER 12: INCOMING

I walked off the boat still rattled and adrenaline in my veins. First thing that hit me was the foul aroma of SHIT. DAMN WAS IT STRONG. As if there were a landfill on fire. DISGUSTING. Concertina wire surrounded the entire base camp at "Cua Viet." Sandbagged bunkers were spaced out and lined the perimeter. All manned 24 hours a day, all armed with M-60 machine guns. I could see a tall tower used as an observation post. Even though its name was CAMP KISTLER, nobody called it that. All Marines called it "Cua Viet." Tall pine trees littered the entire base. There were trails used as walkways. They all were lined with wooden ammo crates. This made it much easier to walk on than the sand. The sand was a light, tan colored. There were brown colored "hooches" that were spread out all over. A hooch was a small A-shaped house that served as our living quarters. They were fortified with an abundance of sandbags to shield us from rocket attacks. They usually held around 15-20 men per one.

I was now part of H&S CO, 1ST AMTRAC battalion, 3RD Marine Division. There were many platoons of Amtracs or "AmGrunts" as we were called. That stood for Amtrac Grunt. An AMTRAC was basically a big tank. These tanks were amphibious and could float on water. They were used to cross the Cua Viet River. We crossed by boats as well. We were on the South side of the river. They usually could carry 15-20 inside. Sometimes they carried Marines on top of it as well. When you reached your final stopping point, the ramp in the back would drop. Marines could disperse quickly from both port and starboard sides.

I got to the Company Headquarters hooch and reported to the 1st Sgt for duty. I was told I would be a part of the "Battalion Scouts." I was assigned to their hooch down the end of the base. He pointed to the direction of the Battalion Scouts hooch and said "CARRY ON." Once I located the hooch, I walked inside. I saw a tall, white Marine with Sergeant stripes. He got off the edge of his cot. I dropped my bag and said "LANCE CORPORAL MOLINA REPORTING FOR DUTY SERGEANT." He replied" I'M SERGEANT KALESNICK, WELCOME TO THE NAM MOLINA."

Sgt Kalesnick issued me a cot and told me to leave my gear. I had to go get ammo at the armory, new weapon, and gear I needed. Still an M-14 was being used. I loved that weapon. Once I got back, Sgt Kalesnick told me I'd have to get schooled on a few things before going out on patrol. I met a few of the scouts there. One of them stood up. He introduced himself as Private First Class, Steve Sandor Sarossy. He was Hungarian. He'd become my best friend in Vietnam. In the days following, I was taught map reading, common booby traps in NAM, hand signals, what to look for, etc. We did a lot of PT daily. I was taught what to do when you hear that word "INCOMING." SHHHIIITTTTTTTT!!!!!!!

INCOMING was the word a Marine would SCREAM once we were being attacked by rocket fire. Everyone would go to a place of safety and run for cover. This usually was near the bunkers that were lined with sandbags. Other than that, you had no cover. A seasoned Marine passed by me. I asked if he was heading to chow and he said he was. I followed him to the chow hall. From our hooch, it seemed like a hike. At least an eighth of a mile. Long walk just to go eat. After a few days of this, another Marine and I were coming back from the chow hall. CHARLIE must've had his dinner early and was ready to rock. A gut-wrenching scream from a Marine finally came that evening. It got EVERYBODY'S attention. He yelled "INCOMMINNNNNNG."

We were caught out in the open and hid behind a pine tree. Just about then enemy rockets started impacting west of our position. They were fired across the Cua Viet River on the North side. Man, the sounds of the rockets impacting were frightening! You could hear the "CRUUUUMP" sound as they hit the sand. I saw one hooch get blown to shits. It was literally vaporized in two seconds. I told the Marine next to me that I could hear a rocket coming. I remember saying "HOLY SHIT I HOPE THAT ONE DON'T HIT US." His reply is forever stenciled in my head. He said" the ones you hear aren't going to hit you. Don't worry about those. Fear the ones that you CAN'T hear. If you can't hear them, they're right on top of you. THEN YOU'RE FUCKED."

A few minutes later it was over. Just like that. It was a lesson from there on that never left my memory. I stopped going to the chow hall after that. I'd rather eat "C-RATS" as they were called, in our hooch. "C-RATS" stood for CANNED RATIONS." Some had turkey, pork, chicken, etc. The best thing to get was a can of peaches and pound cake. It was better than finding money in a can, lol. I'd rather eat out of those cans than being caught out in the open again. I never walked to the chow hall again. Why you ask? Two words: SCARED SHITLESS!

About a week later, Sgt Kalesnick called all of us scouts inside the hooch. He told us he'd be "rotating" back to the States. His time in Vietnam was over. He'd reached DEROS. This stood for (Date Estimated to Return from Overseas). Cute little acronym of the military. It was one everyone talked about. Some would count their days down and others wouldn't. I never did to be honest with you. I didn't want that weight hanging over my neck. The way I saw it was like this: WHEN YOUR TIME IS UP, YOUR TIME IS UP."

As scouts our objective was to do "recon" or reconnaissance patrols. We'd stealthy move out and search for CHARLIE. Both on the South and across the river on the North side. We were not to engage the enemy unless it was absolutely necessary. When we located the enemy, we'd radio their position into Company Headquarters. Once they got the coordinates from us, they'd relay that information to artillery. The Navy gunships floating off the Gulf of Tonkin would get those coordinates too. Along with artillery, the Navy would fire those 16-inch guns and pound the shit out of the enemy.

Fighter jets or "fastmovers" as we called them, would be the icing on the cake. They'd drop napalm all over the obliterated area. There'd be NOTHING alive after that. I mean NOTHING. We were very critical in locating and destroying the enemy. Once this occurred, CHARLIE would send out a few platoons to recon the destroyed area themselves. They'd been hit hard. They knew they had visitors. They knew somebody was close by calling in those artillery and Navy strikes. They weren't fooled. By then, we'd be gone by then.

Our new squad leader came in to replace Sgt Kalesnick. His name was Sergeant Ron Kovic. A white, gung-ho Marine from

Massapequa, New York. He was beginning his second tour. He was high strung and always wanted to train. He constantly talked about his dream of winning the Medal of Honor. That or getting wounded in combat so he could go home a "war hero" as he described it. I NEVER wanted either of those. I just wanted to do my best in the unit and carry my own weight. I didn't want to screw up or get anyone in my unit injured and or killed. I'd rather die than allow that to happen. Staying alive was priority number one in my book.

The Battalion Scouts consisted of these ten men: Kovic, Fant, Rhodes, Perna, Kleppen, Farmer, Sarossy, Beeson, Evans, and myself. We continued to operate on both sides of the Cua Viet River. Sometimes we'd come upon a sizeable force of NVA or VC. We'd call it in and they be blasted into the Stone Age. Other times it was just like a walk in the park. Quiet, peaceful, and nothing out of the ordinary. We'd come back to Cua Viet and drop our gear. After a long ass patrol, the last thing you wanted to do was train more. But we did. Kovic was hard and he would have us doing PT, map reading, etc. We just wanted to rest but there was rarely down time with him. He meant well but at the time it was like torture.

I believe it was late October or early November of 1967, Kovic came inside our hooch. We were told to saddle up and get ready to move out. We'd be going on a night patrol South of the Cua Viet. There were reports of a "sapper battalion" lurking in the neighboring villages or "villes" as we called them. Sappers were members of CHARLIE's team who would sneak inside the perimeter. They'd launch satchel bags full of explosives and blow the whole base to shits.

They were very crafty. In essence, the NVA and VC's "special forces" if you will. They loved doing satchel charges on our ammo dumps too. Blow the ammo dump and our supply is dwindled to nothing. They'd lead a "sapper charge" after knowing we'd be in short supply of ammo.

Another tactic of Sappers was to turn our claymore mines around towards our position. A claymore mine was a horizontally shaped. They have folding legs to push into the ground and make it stable. They were usually olive drab green or grey in color. These were laid out around the perimeter.

They contained over 700 steel balls. A little bigger than pellets but not too much. Internally it contained a layer of C-4 explosive. They are attached to a clacker via wire and blasting cap. When the troop that holds the clacker squeezes it three times, it ignites the mine forward in a 60-degree radius. It is effective up to 100 meters. Once the mines were turned around, they'd be facing the inside of the American perimeter. A sapper would pull the wire on the perimeter or make noise. The soldier or Marine on guard would blow the claymores knowing it was CHARLIE most likely. You'd end up blowing your own comrades up including yourself. Basically, it's like a huge shotgun blast going off. DEADLY. Anything in the "kill zone" instantly turned into hamburger meat. BOOM!

Getting back to the foul aroma of shit permeated throughout the base, I found it came from our outhouse aka the "shitters." There was a hooch with six holes on a wooden plank. It looked like a long bench with six holes basically. You would sit side by side taking a piss or shit seated. Below each whole was a 55-

gallon drum cut in half. It had handles welded onto each side. In the back, there were six "trap doors." Each one had to be lifted in order to have the drum pulled out. Once the drums were pulled out, diesel would be poured into each drum. They were lit on fire. A few lucky Marines would be stirring this shit with a long metal rod till it became ash. It actually worked too. Nobody was running in line to volunteer for this shit burning detail. Usually it fell to the low man on the totem pole. New guys in general. Yes indeed, I got the privilege of that heinous duty multiple times. After we finished, I looked like I'd been poured with tar. After a week that smell still pierced through my nostrils.

"One of the greatest casualties of the war in Vietnam is the Great Society...shot down on the battlefield of Vietnam"

-Martin Luther King Jr-

CHAPTER 13: THE HUT INCIDENT

Dong Ha was the city about 5 miles to the West of Cua Viet. In order to go to the hospital or see the doctor, you had to take a boat down the Cua Viet River. It seemed like every time a boat passed it would take enemy fire from either North or South of the Cua Viet River. This made a lot of us Marines not go to the doctor if we had a sprain, bad cut, fungus, etc. We'd go get our Corpsman (Marine medic who was a Navy enlisted man) and have him sew up or patch up our wounds. If we had a really bad ailment the Corpsman couldn't fix, we'd have to endure that boat ride with bullets whistling towards us. Other than that, it was always a walk to the Corpsman's hooch for fixing. This didn't require getting shot at.

Another thing that really made me shit was CHARLIE's tactics of playing "peek-a-boo." They were good at doing this in the villes and along the Cua Viet River. They would pop out of a "spider hole" which was a hidden hole in the ground. A gook would spray rounds at our positions and then disappear. It would really have you second-guessing yourself and wondering where the hell these bastards were.

When you found one of these spider holes or tunnels, you'd usually do one thing. Grab a "Willie Pete" (which was a white phosphorus grenade) and yell "FIRE IN THE HOLE." Then you'd launch that grenade in the hole. The gooks had a network of tunnels throughout Vietnam. These tunnels for all hand dug and ran for HUNDREDS of miles. Inside these tunnels, they'd have hospitals, fighting holes, living quarters, and passageways. They also ran along the "Ho Chi Minh Trail." This was a main supply route for CHARLIE. Its tunnels ran into Laos, and Cambodia as well. Verified facts!

I got a beautiful letter from my Mother Genoveva. I believe it was November of 1967 and I was getting used to life in Vietnam. My home was the Cua Viet and I did my best to adjust. I never wrote home very much to be honest. When someone would write me, I'd write back. Other than that, I tried not to give the "world" too much thought. That's what we called the United States when we were in NAM; the WORLD.

Anyways, back to my letter I received from my Mother, she told me she'd heard my friend Manuel Orona was in Vietnam. He grew up with me and lived two blocks away in Pecos, Texas just like me. We went to school together in Pecos. Now he was in a city near the DMZ. She gave my address in Vietnam to Manuel's family. Soon we were writing to each other. I was excited. We were less than 10 miles away from each other in Vietnam. His base was located on a small outpost called "Con Thien." I was in Cua Viet. It felt good to hear and know that Manuel was fighting the same war with me in Vietnam.

I got a letter from Manuel saying he was going to request to go down to Cua Viet to visit me. He had already put it in to his Company Commander. He was attached to the 3rd Marine ,5th Tanks, Alpha Company if my memory serves me correctly. I wrote back and told him I'd be looking forward to it. I waited to hear back from him. Two weeks later, I had three days of "line duty." This is where you manned a bunker alongside the perimeter. It was boring yet you had to keep your eyes peeled. I heard footsteps behind me and peeked out to investigate.

There was Manuel carrying his M-14 smiling. His arms were open and we embraced. "Rodolfo, I can't believe it. Good to see you."

The odds of meeting someone in Vietnam that you grew up was a longshot. Had to be in the millions. In Pecos, I lived on 6th Street and his family lived on 8th Street. CAN YOU BELIEVE THAT? We hung out in the bunker for two days. He manned the post with me and it went by uneventful. No gooks or incoming whatsoever. We talked a lot and he told me he was wounded in July of that year. He'd taken a round to the left shoulder. For that, he was awarded a Purple Heart. That's the medal you receive when a U.S. Serviceman is wounded in combat. Manuel was a radio man type with a special classification. He told me he was always close by the LT (Lieutenant) or the OIC (Officer in Charge). After two days, he had to head back to Con Thien. We embraced and wished each other well. I saw him being whisked away in a boat across the Cua Viet River. I prayed he'd make it home alive. He only had two months left on his tour. I had 12 months to go, lol.

Once off line it was time to go back on patrol and do some scouting. We would be operating some of the Cua Viet. We were warned about heavy enemy presence about 4 "klick" to our South. A "klick" is short for Kilometer. We worked our way up to the respective coordinates given to us by intel. Sappers were well trained and were supposed to be around the ville we were heading to. We were at the edge of a small ville. It was raining hard. We were miserable and soaked. Dark as hell too. We laid prone near the rice paddy dikes. Concealed in the treeline. It gave us great cover. On this patrol, LT. Smith went out with us. It was uncommon for an officer to go out on patrol. On rare occasions, this did occur.

LT. Smith started going over to talk to Sgt Kovic. They chatted in the darkness and then called for a few scouts to get a closer look. After that two scouts were ordered to get a closer look. I believe it was Kleppen and Fant. I NEVER left the treeline. Once they returned back from their recon, someone said something like "do you see the sappers carrying satchel bags? They're getting away fire at them." I couldn't see anybody carrying satchels. Right at that moment, one of the scouts started firing. Thinking we were under attack, we all followed suit. I was new and scared out of my mind. We fired on anything that moved. We lit that ville UP!!! When the firing stopped, I remember LT. Smith shouting "how many sappers did we kill?"

Next thing I saw was Sgt Kovic and Kleppen following LT. Smith to the ville. We all followed behind. My adrenaline was PUMPING. We were all wondering what they were going to discover inside those village huts. They came out and Kleppen said "Someone call a medevac helicopter." A scout I can't recall excitedly asked "how many sappers did we hit?" Kleppen responded "there are no sappers. Only old men, women and children. Our morale went spiraling downward.

FUCK!!!! My heart hit the dirt and shattered right there in the ville. We'd wrongly fucked up this entire ville. I just couldn't see how this had happened. Kleppen came out of the hut carrying a small child. You could tell it was a boy. He had wounds all over his little body including his legs. Bandages covered the kid almost completely. Once the medevac came in, Kleppen handed the boy to the door gunner. The medevac took off in an instant and the sounds quickly became distant. I turned to Kleppen and said" how bad was it Kleppen?" He responded somberly "Rudy there were body parts ALL OVER THE FUCKIN HUT. We wasted everything. Blood and brain matter everywhere." He walked away shaking his head.

Just then Sgt Kovic told us to saddle up. It was collateral damage and never should've happened. But it did. Sgt Kovic said "Molina you got point." I grabbed myself together and kept on heading South. The scouts and LT Smith followed behind. We went about our evening. You had to become numb about shit like this. Otherwise it'd eat you alive. It still burns in my heart till this very day. Even though I tried deleting that memory out of my head it never leaves me. I'm pressing the POWER button to turn it off. Instead it is on INFINITE REPEAT and never stops playing in my mind. I can't shut it off. That's the best way to describe what I see daily. Even now.

"My brother may go into hell but he won't go alone"

-Anonymous-

CHAPTER 14: MY FRIEND STEVE

My best friend in Vietnam is the reason I am writing today. Steve Sandor Sarossy. His family had emigrated to United States from Hungary. He was Hungarian and lived in Fairview Park, Ohio. His family thought it was a great idea for him to join the military. They had escaped Communism in their home country and backed him on his decision 100%. God, when I say his name I'm still rattled with immense pain. Pain because he is my friend I miss most. That guy Steve was such an amazing Marine, an amazing friend. We hung out together all around Cua Viet and when we had down time to rest and relax. I'll tell you the special things that he used to do.

Before we used to go on patrol, he would tell me "Rudy let me give you a hug. You never know what can happen." Here was a guy who made me feel special. I'd never felt that kind of love, that kind of brotherhood. I was a new guy so I'd usually walk point. Point man was usually the first one to snag a booby trap, trip wire, or get hit with enemy fire from CHARLIE. It was war and death would take the first man who screamed.

Knowing that I'd get that hug from Steve, it almost put me at ease. It was like it put me on ice. Some guys smoked grass to calm their nerves. I never did that only once. It didn't work out too well, lol. I used to hear that Marines say that Marines were brothers forever. Once I joined and was in Vietnam, I realized the velocity of that statement. So damn true. Steve and I ate together, laughed together, cried together, and promised to meet up once we rotated back to the World.

A former Marine wrote this poem for my friend Steve. That's the exact title: MY FRIEND STEVE. It takes you into my soul and how I feel to this day. Miss you brother. When its my turn to go to Heaven, I hope to see you standing guard at the pearly gates. I never got to tell you and thank you enough. Love you brother Steve. You're in my everyday thoughts.

MY FRIEND STEVE

We were serving proudly in the United States Marines,

That's where I met my best friend Steve.

In a tropical Southeast Asian country 10,000 miles away from home called Vietnam,

Fighting a fierce war in cities with weird names like Dong Ha and Khe Sanh.

We were part of a 10-man Scout team with the Amtracs,

Conducting recon patrols deep in enemy territory while watching each other's backs.

We were called "Battalion Scouts "operating near the DMZ,

Death always lurking around every rock, corner, and tree.

Then came the day we were patrolling in a village called "My Loc" near the Cua Viet River,

The date was January 20th 1968; the most horrible day I'll always remember.

Caught out in the open sand dunes we were ambushed by a battalion size NVA,

Thirteen Marines including Steve would die that fateful day.

Fifty years later, I wish I could pick up the phone and give Steve a call,

Now when I want to talk to him, I have to travel to the Vietnam Wall.

He's located at Panel 34 E,

I touch his name on the black granite wall and my soul starts to bleed.

My best friend from Fairview Park, Ohio, PFC Steve Sandor Sarossy,

Who would give me a hug before I walked point and say "you never know what can happen Rudy."

The Battle of My Loc will forever tell the courage and bravery displayed by our fallen Marines,

I miss you everyday brother, my hero, my friend Steve.

By Adrian M Nunez -USMC-

"Yea, though I walk in the valley of the shadow of death, I will fear no evil; for you are with me; your rod and your staff, they comfort me"

-Psalm 23:4-

CHAPTER 15: NATIONAL SATAN's DAY

JANUARY 20TH 1968. The day that is THEE WORST DAY OF MY LIFE. For many others who were with me operating in the village of My Loc, it too is their worst. The bloody evil and destruction that fell right on top of that tiny village My Loc was relentless. Located just North of the Cua Viet River. That overcast day he would unleash the gates of hell onto the AmGrunts and Battalion Scouts. The Grim Reaper was hungry and his appetite for devastation was at his peak.

Intel had reports that was a huge buildup of NVA troops near the village of My Loc. The talk of the whole base was CHARLIE's plan to launch simultaneous attacks on U.S. strongholds. TET was a Vietnamese holiday and almost 10 days away. Everyone was on high alert and since we were close to the DMZ, we knew it would hit us first more than likely. I remember Sgt Kovic being called to the Command BUNKER. It was a huge command bunker fortified with a ton of sandbags. Once he returned to our hooch, he told us to saddle up and load heavy. We'd be meeting CHARLIE and his pals. All ten of us BATTALION SCOUTS were the first to go. We'd do reconnaissance in front of everyone else once we were on the Northern bank of the Cua Viet near My Loc. Something told me this wouldn't be a good day. I was right.

We headed across the river and headed West towards My Loc via Amtrac. Once we unloaded and hit the greyish sand of My Loc, we headed along the tree line. We had been told a large enemy force was in the village and we needed to find out how many. Being scouts, our job was to avoid any detection whatsoever. We were to report what our findings were. Once we found the gooks, we'd have their positions blown to pieces by artillery and Navy gunships.

Sgt Kovic had us walking in a single file column. There we were, slithering along the treeline, looking for any signs of CHARLIE. I was the eighth man amongst the 10-man column. It seemed eerie in a sense, like quiet. Maybe a little too quiet. Just then, I heard an earth-shattering CRACK! It was like something blew up next to my ear. I looked to my right and noticed a tree branch broken off. It was at the same level as my head. I yelled out "SNIPER." We all went down for cover. I knew the round came from my right. Maybe my "2 o'clock" I'd say. The next thing that happened just didn't make sense. It never has to this day. Sgt Kovic told us to get up and form on a line formation. We were going to do a frontal assault to flush out the sniper. We had absolutely ZERO cover. We were in the open sand dunes. THIS WENT AGAINST SCOUT PROTOCOL. SCOUTS NEVER WALKED OUT IN THE OPEN. EVER!

At THIS point, I knew we were FUCKIN DEAD MEAT. I had no idea why we'd been put here. The next thing we were told by Sgt Kovic was to move forward towards the graveyard directly in front of us. Pagodas were off to the right of the graveyard. The treeline laid directly behind the graveyard.

My heart was THUMPING out of my chest. Man, I'm FUCKIN DEAD. WAAAAAAY TOO SILENT. The only thing you could hear is our gear jingling with each step we took. About 25 meters in, the Gates of Hell opened up on us. The rocket and mortar fire sizzled and shrieked all around us. Small arms and machine gun fire sailed our way by the thousands. Automatic fire by the truckload. Snipers opened up on our position from different angles. The graveyard and the front dune directly ahead of us was taking a pounding. Their forward observer hadn't adjusted his rounds yet. If he did, we'd be FRIED CHICKEN. For some reason they didn't. The earth made the deafening "CRUUUMPP" sounds and lifted the grey My Loc sand high in the air. It came down all around. We'd walked right in an ambush. L-shaped. SHIT!

The hot metal shrapnel whizzing through the air made us hug the sand tight. We continued firing our weapons towards the treeline and the pagodas. The NVA were dug in and bunkers lined the treeline. The NVA their shit together and had us caught out in the open. ZERO cover in sight. No vegetation, no trees, no NOTHING. Sniper fire kept the sand cracking up all around us. They were using the pagodas as cover. My last day on earth is today. I could tell by the intense velocity of the firepower sent upon us. Aint' this a bitch. Also, we had NO CORPSMAN AND NO RADIO. ANOTHER HUGE DEBACLE. WE NEVER PATROLLED WITHOUT THOSE TWO LIFELINES. TODAY WE HAD. CRUCIAL MISTAKE.

Sgt Kovic was to my immediate left. He suddenly rose and the sand CRACKED all around his foot. He fell face first into the sand. It was a violent THUD as his gear made a CRASHING noise. I stopped firing and assessed the situation. Sgt Kovic had been hit in the right foot. It had come out his heel and blown it almost completely off. I had to get on my hands and knees to pull his boot off. Exposing myself out towards the enemy. More rocket fire POUNDED our position and snipers were keying on our position. As I bandaged up Sgt Kovic's foot, I could hear his

M-16 cracking. He was still firing his rifle and in the battle. We were TOTALLY PINNED DOWN. NOWHERE TO GO. NO COVER!

I'll never forget while I was taking his boot off, Sgt Kovic told me" Rudy if we make it outta here alive, I'm going to recommend you for the Silver Star." I almost fell on my ass when I heard that! SILVER STAR? FUCK THE SILVER STAR, WE ARE GOING TO HAVE AN NVA BAYONET WITH A "DEATH CARD" STUCK IN OUR NECKS AT THIS RATE! I couldn't believe he said that. I was FLOORED. Medals weren't on my mind nor were they ever. I was trying to stop the bleeding on his foot. Once I bandaged his foot, I kept firing my M-16 which we recently had for a month now. They were lighter weight and fairly new. Kovic continued to shout obscenities at the gooks as he fired his M-16 towards the pagodas and treeline. The other scouts were to my extreme left firing from the treeline where we came in initially as a column. Farmer was to Sgt Kovic's immediate left. AGAIN, ITS NOT LIKE WE COULD CALL FOR HELP OR CALL IN ARTILLERY. We don't even have a FUCKIN RADIO! We'd later find out that we'd ran into the 803rd North Vietnamese Army (NVA) Regiment.

I continued to fire my weapon as the sand continually CRACKED and rockets kept THUMPING on the earth nearby. I'm going to die, you're FUCKED RUDY! At least these were my thoughts. I heard a loud THUMP that was super close. I saw Sgt Kovic hit in the shoulder as blood EXPLODED in the air. It ran down his flak jacket as he fell backwards. He landed FLAT on his back. His rifle dropped in the sand next to him.

The enemy round had tore through his shoulder and exited through his spinal cord. It shattered it to pieces and left him paralyzed. AHHHHH SHIT, Sgt Kovic is hit again. I stopped firing and once again got on my hands and knees to take off his flak jacket. The volley of rounds increased all around me. I put a battle dressing bandage on his shoulder and told him to hang on. His eyes were rolling into the back of his head. He kept on moaning and groaning. He was done. His war came to an end right there in the middle of that sand dune. Kovic and I were out in the open by our lonesome. The other scouts continued to fire but were too far to help us. Plus, the treeline gave them some sort of cover. If they tried, they'd be mowed down most likely by machine gun fire or snipers. Rockets and mortars started to POUND closer to our position. I had to do something or we BOTH WERE DEAD. We had been in the "kill zone" way too long.

I started to drag Kovic to a small mound to provide us some cover. The enemy fire continued and I'd stop to let off a few rounds towards the treeline where the enemy was dug in. I wanted to make let them know we weren't finished. I was hoping I could hold them off till we got reinforcements to assist our grim situation. If they decided to make a frontal assault, we'd all be going home in body bags. They just kept sending rounds, rockets, and mortar fire by the waves. I continued dragging Kovic until we reached the mound. FINALLY, we had some cover. Farmer appeared to my left and was firing too. He yelled out a second later "AHHH SHIT THEY SHOT MY FUCKIN FINGER OFF."

I made my way away from the mound and assessed Farmer's wound. He had a severed index finger on his firing hand(right). I bandaged his hand up and he started firing from his left hand.

When he was out of ammo, he made a run for it back to our "12 o'clock." There laid a huge SAND BERM. It was called the Razorback. I could see the gooks trying to flank me on my left side. I quickly took aim through my sights as sand continued to CRACK and RAIN on Kovic and I. I saw a few gooks fall to my left. I had wasted them trying to flank me. All the while I checked on Kovic. He was still slipping in and out of consciousness. I waited for my enemy round to hit me any second. It was inevitable. It was definitely the Devil's day. He showed that clearly with the amount of death unleashed on us.

I fired to my left flank, front, and the pagodas. Still firing in all directions came my way. I squeezed my M-16 and heard a click sound. I looked at the bolt and it was WIDE OPEN. FUCK, I WAS OUT OF AMMO. WHAT THE HELL AM I GONNA DO? Now I couldn't protect myself or Sgt Kovic. I fixed bayonet and waited for the gooks to come finish us off. I planned to jab at least a few in the eye before I met my demise. I was hoping it'd be quick. FUCK WE WERE DONE. WE NEEDED HELP OR IT WAS A WRAP.

I peaked my head around the mound and could see the gooks coming forward. Not fast but they were advancing. They must've known we were out of ammo or thought we were dead. Either way I needed ammo or a wave of reinforcements BAD. God answered my prayers at that moment. I saw a Marine land right next to my right side. Once again rockets started CRUNCHING around us. The Marine had his head in the sand. I went to check on him. Once I made my way to the Marine, I asked him if he was ok. I turned him over and could see he was dead. Wounded from an enemy round to the heart. Blood made the sand turn a dark reddish color. I looked at his dog tags around his neck. It said L Cpl Parker. I took his bandoleers of ammo and joined the fight once again. I nailed two gooks running towards the graveyard. One round hit the first one directly in the head. I saw his head come apart into PIECES. Motherfuckers were going to PAY! I WANTED AND WAS TRYING TO WASTE THEM ALL.

Cpl John Keaveney (a tall white Marine), appeared to my LEFT next to Kovic. He raised up firing his rifle and ended up killing three NVA snipers. They had been perched behind the pagodas. The volume of fire from the pagodas decreased DRAMATICALLY after that. He killed a few other NVA soldiers before taking on the hard task. To carry out Sgt Kovic to safety. I could tell the Marines he brought as well as the ones at the Razorback delivered cover fire. It was now or never. He had charged at the pagodas. AMAZING.

Marines at the Razorback started to produce much more firepower towards the enemy treeline. I suspected more men had come to our aid. At that point I could see a few men a little behind me to my right firing. Then I witnessed probably the most COURAGEOUS ACT EVER! Cpl Keaveney ran towards Kovic's position. He laid down and picked up Kovic fireman carry style. All in ONE SWOOP. I could see Kovic's gaping wound as he was wrapped around Keaveney's back. That hole was HUGE and I figured he was dead. I could see Keaveney and Kovic disappear to the safety of the Razorback. I later learned Keaveney had been wounded too. He was later awarded the Silver Star for his actions and conspicuous gallantry. He also received the Vietnamese Cross of Gallantry. Heroic actions on his part. A true HERO! I'LL NEVER FORGET THE BRAVERY and UNCOMMON

VALOR Cpl Keaveney displayed that day. A TRUE DEFINITION OF A U.S. MARINE.

Fire intensified now from both sides. Enemy and friendlies. I fired my rifle and hit a sniper near the pagoda. I could tell I hit him in the chest as he flew back violently. I used Parker's body as cover as I fired my rifle. BAM one more NVA soldier fell dead. One more squeeze and "POP" GOES THE BOLT. Parker's ammo had kept me in the fight and alive. Now I was out of ammo AGAIN. I scanned the area once again. I was all alone. The Kill Zone was hungry for more. I didn't want to become the Grim Reaper's next victim. FUCK! Rounds were impacting Parker's body as I laid against him for cover. It's all I had.

The NVA started to adjust mortar fire and one sailed directly in front of me. "CRUUMMMPPP" is all I heard. Shrapnel screaming with pain sailed over my head. Fuck I have to do something. I could hear the Marines at the Razorback telling me when they started to fire to start running towards them. This was going to be my only chance to get out of that "Kill Zone." Time to get the hell outta Dodge. Time to stare death directly in the face. I had now been out in the open pinned down for 30-45 minutes. It felt more like a LIFETIME.

I remember this clearly like it was yesterday. I grabbed one of Parker's dog tags off his person. I put them in my pocket. I said a prayer and said "God if I have to die, just make it a head or heart shot so I don't feel anything." Once I heard the Marines fire the first round, I jumped up and began zig zagging to the safety of the berm. I was SCREWED......I could hear death calling my name.

I could hear the fire get worse from both sides. Bullets were being fired from my front by the Marines at the berm (Razorback). I had what seemed like a hundred rounds fired from the enemy to my rear. They all had my name "RUDY MOLINA" on each of those enemy rounds. I kept zig zagging and once I was halfway to the Razorback, I started to see a glimmer of hope. C'mon God, just let me reach that berm. I hauled ass even faster and a burst of energy shot through my feet. I was almost at the berm. C'mon feet, MOVE FASTER I THOUGHT.

Once I was close enough, I did an Olympic type jump and DOVE into the berm. FINALLY, after all this time it was OVER. I was in the safety of my Marine brothers. I grabbed some bandoleers of ammo and took cover on the edge of the berm. I wondered how the scouts in the treeline were doing. I wanted to make my way over there but there was no way I'd make it alive. This PISSED ME OFF knowing I couldn't reach my fellow scouts. It was a sick feeling to be honest. I reloaded my M-16 and continued to engage.

I had heard an Amtrac off to my right side the whole time I was pinned down. I never saw it though. My face was buried in the sand and I only came up to fire on the enemy. Just to let them know we were still in the fight. I could see where the Amtrac was now from the Razorback. The casualties must've been huge. The Amtrac had driven up to the NVA bunkers almost running them over. LT. Reynolds had been in charge of that Amtrac. I'd later learn that was 3rd platoon of Alpha Company. According to survivors there, they were decimated to nil in less than five minutes.

I asked the RTO (Radio Transmitting Operator) who was at the Razorback what the status was with the Battalion Scouts. I was worried about Steve and the others. He yelled back at me that another Amtrac had gone to retrieve them. When it finally pulled in the Razorback, I saw Steve laying on a stretcher. His guts were practically hanging out of his stomach. His eyes were wide open. He had been almost cut in half by enemy fire. He was dead. The worst day of my life. Four Scouts were WIA (Wounded in Action) and one KIA (Killed in Action). Other Scouts and AmGrunts have given their accounts of that day also. Here is what Scout Dennis Kleppen witnessed that day:

KLEPPEN: Sometime around late morning, Sgt Kovic was called to the Command Bunker. He returned and ordered us to get our gear and saddle up. Someone passed out extra bandoleers of ammo and grenades. We heard some talk of a battle progressing near the DMZ. The mood was very somber. The Scouts were ready as always. Nobody knew that today was the beginning of a large communist offensive that would be the last for many Marines.

Boarding Tracs' we began our journey. Crossing the river, we started to head North. Less than a klick up the coast the Tracs' turned inward. Soon they stopped and we all dismounted. Kovic went to a meeting and returned in short order. During this wait thoughts of what lay ahead passed my mind. Will it be quick and painless? Will I lay in the dirt mortally wounded, my life's blood slowly oozing from me through hundreds of shrapnel holes? Will I be blinded, lose an arm or a leg, or be paralyzed for the rest of my life? Kovic told us we'd lead a sweep across the graveyard and an open area into the treeline along the East side of Jones Creek. This would be to take care of any enemy we came in contact with.

The Marines that came with us would be on line behind us. At least that's what we were told. As we moved out, I noticed we didn't have a radio operator. STRANGE. VERY STRANGE. More thoughts. Maybe an artillery round will land in my back pocket and settle the question once and for all. No radio, no Corpsman, no reinforcements. We all knew today was going to be a bitch. We broke out of the West end of the ville. Kovic told us to get in line and advance. Kovic was doing all kinds of hand and arm signals to get us in a straight line from North to South.

On line we were, 1st Amtrac Battalion Scouts with Kovic strutting in the lead. Just like General Patton himself shouting something about killing those commie bastards. It's so God damn quiet you could hear your gear shifting as you walked through the sand. No noise from the ville to our South and the ville directly ahead of us. No movement anywhere but the Scouts. Something ain't right. We're in deep shit. Then the DOOR OF HELL OPENED!

Machine guns, AK-47's, RPG'S (Rocket Propelled Grenades), antiaircraft weapons, recoilless rifles, you name it. It was all coming our way in a wave of blind death not caring who was in its path. Instinctively, we returned fire and dove to the ground looking for cover. There was NO COVER AT ALL. Caught in the open we were. We couldn't have been more visible if someone had painted large red bullseyes on us.

Miraculously, we all survived the initial burst. Bullets flew by us as the sharp crack told you that they were within a hairs' breath of striking flesh; my flesh. No screams for a Corpsman. Not that it would've done any good. We didn't have one. All we had was each other, first aid kits, and atropine. Kovic was hit in the foot, heel to be exact, during the initial exchange. We returned fire towards our front. Whenever one of us raised up to fire it was like waving a red flag in front of a bull, a MAD BULL.

Rounds of every type from everywhere cut through and were impacting anything in its path. The sharp CRACK of round sent chills up and down my spine. Damn them, they had us dead to rights. All of us were going to die. Kovic will get us all killed for sure, not just one or two of us. Kovic stood up and started moving towards the enemy shouting obscenities at them. He shouted at the Scouts to get up and charge. We were Marines and should fight like Marines. Yes, we were. It didn't take a rocket scientist to figure out that none of us would get ten feet if we stood up and charged. We were less than a dozen against HUNDREDS. AN ATTACK WAS SUICIDAL.

We continued to exchange fire. The enemy forces concentrated their fire on whoever fired at them. Kovic was down, hit again by an enemy round. To see a body jerk, at the same time clothing, flesh, and blood, move rapidly away from the body. It happens so quickly but seeing it in action seems to take forever. It is forever, forever SEARED in my mind. The sounds of artillery rounds exiting the tube suddenly filled the air. It was coming from the North and that meant NVA artillery. SHIT. I hoped they were firing at the Cua Viet. They weren't. As if we didn't have enough trouble, incoming was headed our way. The first volley of fire was landing short. GOOD. Fortunately, our small numbers resulted in no casualties from these initial barrages but God shook the earth. Shrapnel screamed through the air and the smell of burnt gun powder filled our nostrils. It made you take short breaths.

About this time, Ron Farmer took a round to the hand. A bullet had struck him on his right trigger finger. I heard him say something like "they shot me in the damn finger" or of that sorts. A couple of scouts made their way to Kovic and tended to him. Farmer's hand was bandaged and he continued to engage the enemy firing with his other hand. There were so many of them we didn't have to be choosy about where we fired.

The battle continued. NO FUCKING RADIO, can't call supporting fire or a medevac. We're just plain SCREWED! More incoming rounds fell upon and I prayed my name wasn't on any of them. WHAM! What used to be a small mound about ten feet away was now flat ground. SHIT. TOO DAMN CLOSE. We were lucky but we were holding our own.

Cpl Beeson took up a team and headed for the ville. This was to block any NVA trying to maneuver to our left flank. As they were leap frogging thru the ville, they came under heavy enemy fire. At some point, Beeson was shot in the ass. Right butt cheek to be exact. He was lucky to have survived.

As Steve Sarossy took the gun emplacement under fire, he was wounded. He died shortly after from his wounds he sustained. His fellow Scouts surrounded him as he passed away. Then I heard a noise from the East. They were Tracs (AMTRACS). They stopped suddenly. What was going on? Who is back there? When we came inland, most of the Battalion was heading North.

Friendlies now were at the rear. Another Scout and I were closest to the left. We were ordered to go and get help. Crawling, running, and moving towards the treeline till we finally made it. Crossing an opening we found friendlies on line behind the treeline. We gave them a quick report and asked for help. We took a brief drink of water and reloaded empty magazines. We couldn't get back to our pinned down Scouts any faster. Grabbing extra bandoleers of ammo, we rushed back out to help.

We dispersed ammo to everyone left who was running short. I could only imagine the pain Ron was in. We continued to engage the NVA. No artillery support, just NVA artillery sailing our way. We were so "punch drunk" it didn't bother us anymore. Unless it REALLY CAME CLOSE. SHIT. More incoming. WAIT! THAT'S OURS! By God its about time. Give em' hell. WHOOPIE! I glanced to my right and saw a Trac full of Marines. They were headed straight towards the enemy. They just kept going. I laid my head on my rifle and said: GOD NO! NO! STOP THEM! They didn't get much farther. They NVA opened up on them quickly. Some died quickly. Others didn't. It was a fight for survival. The cries of the wounded are forever etched in my head; the volume is stuck on HIGH.

The Battle for control of Cua Viet River raged on for days after. We were rescued by reinforcements and all made it back to the berm. Dead bodies were transported to the rear and severely wounded were medevac'd. Marines were brought in from all over and eventually the NVA were driven out. They suffered massive casualties on their end. We paid a heavy price. Every man who took part that day and the days that followed were changed FOREVER.

MOLINA: I lost track of time after that. Seeing all the wounded in the rear fucked my mind up. Especially seeing Steve's dead body on the stretcher. The bag of immense PAIN AND SADNESS that his parents would receive when they opened their door in Ohio. Greeted by a Marine in dress blues to tell them that their son was dead. FUCK, I couldn't imagine that shit. 12 other AmGrunts' parents would get that same "death notice." I was spinning in a world of chaos. I couldn't focus whatsoever. The adrenaline was wearing off. A wave of GRIEF AND ANGER all rolled in one shot down my throat. It landed DIRECTLY inside my heart. I still can't get rid of that...even today. 51 YEARS LATER.

Another Scout named Gene Perna gives his account of what he saw. He was towards my far left near the treeline. He tells you what he observed from his eyes.

PERNA: I was attached to 1st Amtrac Battalion, 3rd Marine Division. We were part of a 10-man Scout team. BATTALION SCOUTS we were called. On January 20th 1968, we were ordered to recon the small ville of My Loc. Our squad leader was Sgt Kovic. We were assigned an RTO, Cpl Lattone. When we dismounted from the Trac, Sgt Kovic and Cpl Lattone met with Alpha Company for a briefing. When Sgt Kovic returned, the radio man was gone.

We were to recon the ville of My Loc. Sgt Kovic ordered us on line facing the village. We started to walk across the sands without any cover. About 45 meters in, we came under intense automatic weapons and sniper fire. We all dropped to the prone position but Sgt Kovic was hit in the foot first. PFC Steve Sarossy was severely wounded in the stomach and fell. We returned fire but the fire was so intense we couldn't move. We had NO cover.

L Cpl Rhodes and I went to Sarossy to attend to his wounds. Just then, Rhodes was shot in the right hand and dropped his M-79 grenade launcher in the sand. Sarossy abdomen was wide open and his entrails were coming out. I bandaged up Rhodes' hand and noticed all the Scouts on the left flank had extracted themselves. L Cpl Molina was up on his hands and knees taking Sgt Kovic's boot off to bandage it up. L Cpl Farmer was talking to Kovic who was moaning in pain. L Cpl Farmer was shot in the right hand and his trigger finger was severed. Cpl Beeson had took a round in the buttocks.

L Cpl Molina immediately bandaged up Farmer's right hand. Farmer continued firing from his left hand. Molina was firing also. The Tracs and Army helo began strafing the NVA in the treeline and the ville to our front. This gave Beeson and Farmer time to extract themselves out of the open. We still were taking sniper fire but not as intense. Sgt Kovic was hit again and began to moan loudly. I saw L Cpl Molina stop firing and get up to take Sgt Kovic's flak jacket off. He started to bandage his wound all the while exposed to sniper fire. Bullets hitting close to him but he continued bandaging Sgt Kovic's shoulder.

He drug him to a small sand berm that provided a little bit of cover. Sarossy and I started to say an Act of Contrition together and he expired right next to me. I returned fire till I ran out of ammo. I extracted myself out to the safety of the big sand berm where the Tracs were. Alpha Co. Marines ran out to Sgt Kovic and L Cpl Molina's position. L Cpl Molina was still returning fire and protecting Sgt Kovic. Once the Alpha Co Marines extracted Sgt Kovic to safety, L Cpl Molina was still out in the open, taking enemy fire. Once he ran out of ammo, he used an Alpha Co. Marine's ammo (later identified as L Cpl Parker). Parker laid dead in the sand. He continued to fire at the enemy. L Cpl Molina displayed uncommon valor and dedication to his fellow Marines that day. He exposed himself twice to bandage Sgt Kovic's wounds and also bandaged L Cpl Farmer's hand. All while bullets ripped around him. L Cpl Molina was the last Battalion Scout to make it to safety at the berm.

MOLINA: L Cpl Farmer tells a similar account as L Cpl Perna's. We were FUCKED from the very beginning. War is HELL and that day, January 20th 1968, was and ALWAYS WILL BE THE WORST DAY OF MY LIFE. Everybody who fought that fateful day probably feels exactly the same. That bastard (the devil) had wreaked havoc like none other on us that overcast, January day. I'd later find out Lt. Reynolds' Amtrac took an even worse beating. Out of 30 Marines of 3rd platoon, 12 lost their lives including Lt. Reynolds. Another 11 were wounded. The grey sands of My Loc were turned bloody red all over. Our souls took severe wounds that would last a lifetime. We ALL fought with courage and we NEVER abandoned ANY MARINE. If that was the case, everyone would've made it out unscathed.

"I am not a hero but the brave men who died deserved this honor"

-Ira Hayes-

CHAPTER 16: THEE HONORABLE THIRTEEN

The AmGrunts of 3rd Platoon, A Co. had it much worse that day. As I stated earlier, I never saw an Amtrac. I heard one off to my right. The velocity of fire raining down on our position deafened us. All I knew was the enemy fire came from almost every direction except from our South. One Marine wrote an all-out description of the events that fateful January 20th 1968 day of misery. His name is L Cpl Robert D "Cookie" Cook. Here is his story.

L CPL ROBERT D "COOKIE" COOK: One single day was the worst ever for me. That day was January 20th 1968 and it will always be heavily seared in my memory. I really don't like thinking about it. However, sometimes the memories just flood in like picture frames of a fragmented movie. Even today, I can still recall the events of January 20th, 1968 just like a recently watched movie. Sometimes the images come back to me in flashbacks. They are of things I really wish I'd never seen.

I was one of the lucky who were neither killed or wounded that day. On the eastern edge of My Loc, on the Cua Viet River near its mouth running into the South China Sea. We were known as "AmGrunts" and A Company was constantly used as a rifle company. I loved riding the LVTP-5 A1 Amtracs everywhere we went. Then disembark and leave them behind. We were given the pleasant freedom of patrolling from village to village on foot. When sunset came, we'd set up ambushes.

Everyone did two-hour fire watches then slept for two hours. I honestly enjoyed the patrols and mingling with the village children. We usually would go out on five-day patrols. Once we were done, we'd radio to be picked up by the Tracs.' Then it was back to Cua Viet. Everyone had nicknames. Mine was "Cookie." We were hurried and packed onto one trac. Something was going down in the village of My Loc. Thirty of us were going somewhere in a hurry. Soon there were bullets whizzing over our heads. The noise of the Amtrac motor was extremely loud. I could hear some Marines saying "what the hell is going on?" We all looked at each other realizing things were going to happen soon. Cpl Hank Ralya of Shalimar, Florida was carrying an M-79 grenade launcher. He was directly acroos from me as rounds sailed over our heads. He yelled out" I don't know what the hell is going on but I'm sure ready to kill some gooks."

The NVA regulars had been up in the DMZ since the Spring of 1967. They were highly trained and well disciplined. They wore green pith helmets and green army fatigues. Just then a rocket propelled grenade hit the front of our amtrac. We almost ran over the NVA soldiers who were shooting at us from across the sandy plains. We were under intense rifle and machine gun fire. Some Marines were killed right on top of the Amtrac. We jumped off with many of us landing on each other.

I saw most Marines taking cover behind the Amtrac. I wanted no part of that. It'd be a killing zone and it was. I took my chances and ran to the left of the Amtrac about 60 feet away. I dropped in a prone position in the watery sand. The firing was so intense that most of the killed or wounded occurred within the first three minutes. They were hitting us so close you could see their eyes when they popped up. They were fully equipped and most had AK-47's.

They were right on top of us. They would jump up and fire at us at point blank range. Some of the Marines died instantly. I remember PFC Washington, the strongest Marine in our platoon, staring blankly towards the sky. Shouts for "corpsman" went unanswered as Corpsman Ron "Doc" Blasius was immediately hit and nowhere to be seen.

A Marine next to me took a round through his open mouth and exited out of his neck. He went hysterical and I told him to pick up his rifle and start firing. He kept crawling around screaming "I'M HIT I'M HIT." Cpl Marshall just couldn't control his emotions and was blinded by shock. I couldn't stop to help him though. The firing was just too intense. I kept firing at the numerous NVA soldiers around me. Just about everyone on my left flank was shot.

Lieutenant Reynolds was on top of the berm where the enemy was firing from. He didn't move at all during the battle and raised his right arm briefly. His last words were "GET BACK." He was killed by machine gun fire. PFC Gerald Lenz was shot in the leg and screaming frantically for "HELP." He started turning blue in the face. He realized he was bleeding to death. He started laughing and died laughing in less than two minutes. There was death, bleeding, and chaos all around.

I'd seen several faces of enemy soldiers. One of them was hiding behind a bush and didn't have a helmet or rifle. He just kept looking through the bush which concealed him but provided no cover. I had a perfect head shot at his head. I squeezed off a round and hit him in the forehead. His head exploded. Then a flame of fire shot in the air about 30 feet high. The entire scene played out in slow motion. I had an immediate rush of satisfaction. I got him before he got me. Later we realized the NVA soldier was carrying a flamethrower. It was later recovered.

Cpl Hank Ralya was shooting in the same direction. He was shot and knocked down as he fired his M-79 grenade launcher from a standing position. Ralya immediately got back up on his feet and fired a second time. Then automatic weapons fire hit him again. This completely knocked him down. UNBELIEVABLY, Ralya got back on his feet..a THIRD TIME. Ralya literally died in midair as the heavy volume of fire lifted his body off the ground. This was the most gruesome death that day but there were others. He valiantly died with an M-79 round clenched in his hand.

Private Paul Roberts was lying very still in the sand. The Amtrac was backing up and we all screamed to stop. Roberts was decapitated by the Amtrac backing up. I was sickened by this. The sandy ground was taking mortar fire and I saw mortar shells explode right in front of me. Marines continued to yell and scream. I continued to lie in a prone position keeping my eyes on the sandy berm in front of me. I sometimes fired at the NVA soldiers just to keep their heads down.

Suddenly a Huey gunship came in right on top of us. The door gunner opened up on the NVA soldiers. The gunner never stopped firing with his machine gun going full blast. At times it was no more than 50-75 feet off the ground. The NVA would start firing at the helicopter and you would see it dodging bullets like a bucking bull. Finally, the NVA ceased the heavy firing. It made them fall back. I believe we'd all been killed including the wounded who couldn't move had it not been for that Huey gunship.

Soon Marine artillery came rushing over our heads on NVA positions. They were called in by our RTO, L Cpl Dan Reeves. He'd been shot so badly in the legs he couldn't move. We had driven them back. This time they were the hammer.

MOLINA: As you can imagine, 3rd platoon had taken a pounding just as bad. It goes to show the fierce fighting that took place that day near the village of My Loc. We all ended up back at the Cua Viet. The only thing I remember was being debriefed by Cpt. Hamilton in his hooch. Two days after, I was transferred out. I'd never go back to the Cua Viet ever again. Only in my nightmares and dreams. Etched in my mind and soul. FOREVER.

THEE HONORABLE THIRTEEN'S NAME AND RANK

-PVT PAUL MICHAEL ROBERTS was born on July 8th,1947. He was from South Bend, Indiana. He was killed in action on January 20th,1968.

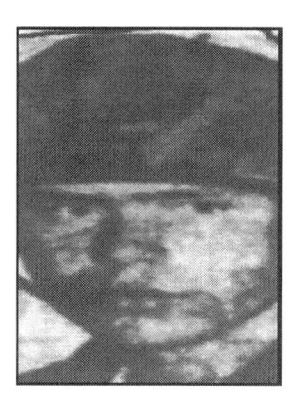

-PFC STEPHEN ANTHONY GUARDINO was on June 3rd, 1948. He was from Norristown, Pennsylvania. He was killed in action on January 20th, 1968.

-PFC GEORGE ARTHUR LINK was born on February 27th, 1948. He was from New Kensington, Pennsylvania. He was killed in action on January 20th, 1968.

-PFC JOHN WASHINGTON was born on April 25, 1947. He was from Earle, Arkansas. He was killed in action on January 20th, 1968.

-2LT RICHARD PETER REYNOLDS was born on September 25,1944. He was from New York, New York. He was killed in action on January 20th, 1968.

-PFC CLARENCE E MITCHELL was born on September 13,1949. He was from Cincinnati, Ohio. He was killed in action on January 20th,1968.

-CPL WARREN HENRY "HANK" RALYA JR was born on October 21st,1946. He was from Shalimar, Florida. He was killed in action on January 20th,1968. He was posthumously awarded the Navy Cross for his actions that day.

-L CPL MICHAEL MCCORD ROSENBERRY was born on June 17th,1948. He was from Marysville, Ohio. He was killed in action on January 20th,1968.

-PFC FRED HAROLD SPEAR was born on July 2nd,1948. He was from Roseville, Michigan. He was killed in action on January 20th,1968.

-LCPL DONALD FREDERICK PARKER was born on May 13th,1946. He was from Dalton, Georgia. He was killed in action on January 20th,1968.

-LCPL RICK DUANE DEEDS was born on July 30th,1948. He was from Carleton, Michigan. He was killed in action on January 20th,1968.

-PFC STEVE SANDOR SAROSSY was born on August 9th,1947. He was from Fairview Park, Ohio. He was killed in action on January 20th,1968. He was my best friend in Vietnam.

-PFC GERALD FRANCIS LENZ was born on April 23rd,1949. He was from Whiting, Indiana. He was killed in action on January 20th,1968.

Stained glass window commissioned by Major Throm.

Inside Chapel at MCRD, Parris Island, SC.

"There is no hunting like the hunting of man, and those who have hunted armed men long enough and liked it, never care for anything else thereafter"

-Ernest Hemingway-

CHAPTER 17: SHORT TIMER STATUS

Once I had left Cua Viet, I fought in the Battles of Khe Sanh and then Hue. Both with Delta Co, 26th Marines, 3rd Marine Division. We were based out of the city of Quang Tri. In Hue, we fought in a place called "the Cathedral." There were massive amounts of gooks there fighting. Viet Cong mainly. Just outside the city of Hue as we rolled into the city, all along the roads I witnessed a horrific sight. DEAD BODIES EVERYWHERE. From grown Vietnamese men, women, and CHILDREN. You could see the bloated bodies of these corpses. The foul aroma of death lingered in the air. It was worth than the shit smelling air in the Cua Viet. That smell is embedded in my brain and never have I endured a worse smell. To this day, it is still there. Among other things I saw in the NAM.

For the next three months, the 26th Marines went fighting everywhere in the Quang Tri Province. We were never stationary and endured more intense fighting. By this time, I had become somewhat numb. If I saw a body blown to pieces, I wouldn't even shake. You had to become stone and forget you ever had feelings. Sounds cutthroat right? It was. It was just what you had to do to survive the NAM. Plain and simple. I still thought of Steve and the 12 others we lost in January at My Loc. I couldn't dwell on it but I'd see Steve's face every night. Sometimes I'd wake up in the field, hearing his voice calling me. "Rudy, come check this out?" I'd go to the tree where I heard the voice. NOTHING. I'd go back to sleep in my hole. Pissed off and sad. The reality of war was you would see the very worst of mankind. I did.

Around April, I was called to the Captain's hooch. We were based in the city of Quang Tri. Captain Cromier told me to have a seat. He started talking. "Molina, you're coming up for R&R (Rest and Relaxation). Have you thought where you wanna go? You have seven days of freedom. Get back at me ASAP." I walked out of the hooch thinking, wow a vacation? I'm going to Bangkok, Thailand.

In Vietnam, you served 13 months of duty. When you reached your six-month mark, you'd get to go on R&R for a whole week. Married men flew to Hawaii to meet up with their wives. It was like the halfway point. Single men like me would go to Bangkok or Australia. I had chosen my destination. I'd be going to Bangkok. This was going to be different and I was hoping for a week of fun. It didn't disappoint.

I hopped on a military plane and landed in a small airbase outside of Bangkok. U.S. jets were often kept there and military personnel. I took a jeep ride into the city of Bangkok. The streets looked like New York City at lunch hour. Bustling with people by the hundreds. The only difference was they were all Asian. I had no rifle and felt very uncomfortable. Once I got to my hotel of chance, I went to a "go-go" bar in downtown Bangkok. These bars offered EVERYTHING from alcohol to sex in a booth. It was HEAVEN.

I sat down in the bar by myself and was immediately courted by 3 Thai women. They were smoking hot and barely had any clothing on. I ordered a beer and started to relax. A few other U.S. Servicemen were sitting a few tables to my right. They all raised their beers up and yelled 'CHEERS." An hour later a hot young Thai woman came and sat on my lap. I'd never had sex with an Asian woman before in my life. That changed that minute. We settled on a price. We went to the back of the bar where cubicles had been set up. We chose one and the rest is history. I felt almost human again. ALMOST I SAID.

One good thing that sticks out more than anything was the music. Man, they were playing all of the music we listened to back in the world. Smokey Robinson, Marvin Gaye, the Temptations, the Dells, etc. It brought me back to Pecos, Texas. I imagined myself in a dance hall watching my brother play the sax with his band Mondie and the Mystics. I immersed myself in that frame of mind and went wild. I was smiling, drinking, and had girlies flocking all around my presence. Who would've thought there was a bloody war going on just a few countries away in Vietnam?

I'd go eat hot food in different restaurants all over Bangkok. I'd bar hop till the wee hours. Sleeping in a bed made me uneasy. I wasn't used to that anymore. I'd wake up and peek out the hotel window. Making sure CHARLIE wasn't going to come in my room and slit my throat while I dreamt of the world. When I would walk the streets, it looked like CHARLIE could be each one. It really fucked my mind up. I tried to relax as best as I could. The fun was now over once my week expired. I thought of pulling a "Manuel Orona" move and "overstay" my R&R. But I didn't. He had done that and it got him demoted. It was hard to go back to war. Some had discipline and others didn't. No shame there. Believe me, I thought of it. I'm not going to lie. Manuel wasn't the only one who pulled that stunt. TRUST ME.

Once back with the 26th Marines, we continued to endure firefights with the enemy frequently. They'd end as fast as they started. The TET offensive lasted from the end of January till April. The Viet Cong was literally wiped out and were never relevant in the Vietnam War again. The survivors went back to life as a fisherman or farmer. Back to their water buffalos and rice paddies they could shit in, lol.

October came in a rush. I was now a "short timer" and was almost at the end of my tour. A few of my Marine brothers started talking about their plans once they rotated back to the world. I hadn't even thought about it. I was in a trance and just lived for Vietnam. I wondered if I even knew how to act around people. Normal people who didn't know what I'd seen through my eyes. In November of 1968, a supply guy from the unit came in my hooch. "Molina, you can check your gear in with me. I'll meet you at the armory. I heard you're leaving tomorrow. Lucky you. Anyways you can catch a jeep to Da Nang tonight." I catapulted off my cot and packed all my shit up. I went to the Captain's hooch and got my orders. Once I had my orders in hand, I went to the armory and turned in my weapon, gear, etc. I was leaving the NAM. I had survived by the Grace of God. It was time to go. 13 months that forever changed my life. Any innocence I had, it died in Vietnam. For many others I'm sure they felt the same way.

"I felt more comfortable getting shot at by the Vietnamese than I did having rotten fruit thrown at me by Americans"

-Anonymous Vietnam Veteran-

CHAPTER 18: DEROS

I was standing on the tarmac on Da Nang airstrip. Many other Servicemen stood with me and they were all smiles. It was almost surreal I'm telling you. I, personally felt like I had a kool-aid smile going from ear to ear. It just hadn't hit me that we were finally going back to the world: DEROS! I used to hear everybody talking about DEROS this and DEROS that. I was understanding what I was all about now. Once we loaded the plane, I took a window seat in the back. I felt the speed picking finally picking up. MAN, I'M GOING BACK HOME. THE WORLD AWAITS.

The plane started to lift up and we were airborne. I could see Vietnam disappearing more and more. I was perfectly fine with that. Once we cleared airspace, I felt at ease. For the first time in 13 months, I let my guard down. The next day after a few stops, I landed in San Francisco, California. My plan was to stop and visit my Aunt Gracie. She lived on the outskirts of San Francisco. I stopped in the airport and located a pay phone. I called my Aunt Gracie and told her I was back. She was excited and told me they awaited my arrival. I grabbed my sea bags and started walking through the airport. People in the airport started snickering at me. I could see the hatred in the eyes of the people. The name calling started to be shouted towards me. "BABY KILLER, GET OUT OF HERE. BRAINWASHED FOOL, YOU'RE NOT WELCOMED HERE. FUCKING IDIOT." Man, I felt like shit. These people knew nothing of the NAM. I WAS THERE, THEY WEREN'T. I walked even faster till I hit the cab line. I couldn't get my bags in the trunk any quicker. The Vietnam War had become very unpopular. This was my "WELCOME HOME." Once

I was in the cab, I felt relieved. Finally, I was heading to my Aunt's house.

I was at the doorsteps of my Aunt Gracie's in an hour. She opened the door and was excited to see me. "RODOLFO, HOW ARE YOU? OH, I'M SOOOOOO HAPPY TO SEE YOU. WOW YOU'RE ALL GROWN UP." My Aunt Gracie fixed me a wonderful meal and we talked extensively. Nothing of Vietnam and I asked her the questions. I didn't want to be asked nothing of that place. Plus, I wanted to hear what was new, what was going on in her life. Anything she wanted to talk about I was fine with that. Just don't ask me of Vietnam. Those were my thoughts and fears.

I was really blown away with the simple things I forgot. I went to the restroom and flushed the toilet. Wow, I looked in amazement like discovering a new toy. Turning on the shower and standing there for what seemed like forever. Our showers were field showers and the water was rarely hot. Vietnam was so damn humid but it would get really cold too. It was crazy. These simple things made me smile and I could feel my life had REALLY changed.

I tried not to act surprised and didn't want anybody thinking I was different. I didn't want them to know what I had did in NAM. To deflect any questions, I did the asking for the most part. You have to understand, I'd felt like I'd became a savage with a savage mentality. There were no rules, no guidelines. Either kill or BE KILLED. I really had to get my head straight. I really thought that would happen overnight. What a fool I was. Maybe it was just the hopes of desperation.

After two days of relaxing in my Aunt Gracie's house, I told her I'd be going home. Finally, I'd be heading back to Pecos. The place I grew up in and had so many memories of. I took a cab to the Greyhound Bus station and bought a one-way ticket to Pecos. I was a long bus rides that endured many stops along the way. Arizona, New Mexico, and finally Texas. I finally reached the Pecos bus station. I took a cab and showed up right there on 6th Street. There was my Mother. Coming outside the door in a mad rush. We embraced and she starting weeping uncontrollably. I felt her worry, her pain, and every other shitty feeling she endured. She never knew how close she came to never seeing me again. I could see her beauty and her love for me. The only unconditional love I've never felt in my life. I surely didn't get that from my Dad. I was happy to be back home in Pecos. I had a 30-day leave until I had to report back to Camp Pendleton in Southern California.

My brother Richard and my sisters came to hug me too. Richard told me he had a gig the next evening and if I wanted to join him. "YEAH I WANNA GO." I loved going to his gigs. I mainly hung around the house and enjoyed all the home cooking my Mother shelled out in the table. It was just so GREAT being in the house again. Listening to my sisters and what was going on in their lives. They all told me how school was going and everyday life in Pecos. I loved hearing their stories and the excitement that flowed in their eyes.

Richard and I were hanging out daily after this. I went over to Pecos High School to visit one of my favorite teachers: Mrs. Graham. She couldn't believe it when I walked through those doors. She was so happy to see me. We had another teacher take a picture of us. I sat down with her and told her I was on leave for 30 days. She showed me a few school projects in her classroom and what changes were made at the school. After about a half an hour, we said our goodbyes and wished each other well. I still have that picture of us today. Good ol' Mrs. Graham.

The remaining 30 days were filled with fun and flew by at blinding speed. Next thing you know, I was saying goodbye to the family once again. Richard took me to the bus station to catch the bus. I would be off to my permanent duty station. This was Camp Pendleton. I was looking forward to going there. It was close by the beach and the surrounding towns were very affluent. Another chapter in my life was about to start. California dreamin' it was.

Our 10 Man Battalion Scout Team.

Christmas Time December 1967, Cua Viet.

Corporal John P. Keaveney. He was awarded the Silver Star and Vietnamese Cross of Gallantry for his actions on 1/20/1968. He is the Marine who carried Sgt. Ron Kovic to safety.

Sgt. Kovic being medevac'd on 1/20/1968.

Down time at Cua Viet

Beeson's "million dollar" wound.

Me at Cua Viet, December 1967.

Marine Brotherhood.

Horse Play.

Watch tower at Cua Viet.

Captured enemy flag.

Captured enemy gear.

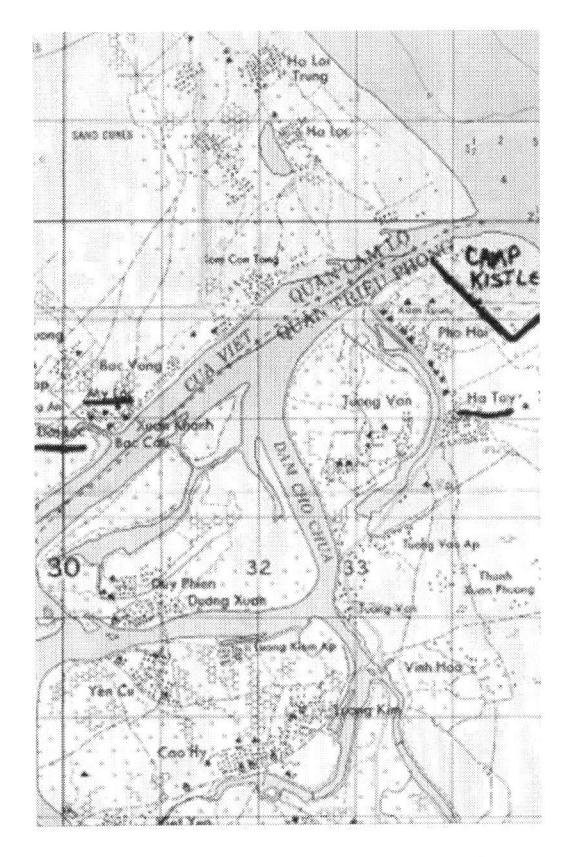

Map of Camp Kistler a.k.a. Cua Viet.

The Cua Viet River was a vital supply route for both sides.

My Loc is to the West. It lies on the North side of the Cua Viet River.

Me in Federal Prison.

My brother Richard.

My daughters Zenia, Gisela, Lynn

and my sister Trine.

Having dinner with Gisela, her husband Anthony

and my granddaughter Ninel.

Duke Cooper, the first to sign

Steve Sarossy's plaque.

The Plaque I made for Steve Sarossy.

102 signatures on the back.

Me at Cua Viet, 2017.

Me in 2017 honoring Steve at My Loc.

Master Gunnery Sgt. Dennis Kleppen and his Wife.

Me and Major Throm in 2017.

Me and my good friend Manuel Orona, 2014.

Fellow scout Ron Farmer and meat my house in Coulterville, CA.

"It is better to create than to learn. Creating is the essence of life"

-Julius Caesar-

CHAPTER 19: SURVIVOR's GUILT

I made my way to Camp Pendleton and got settled in. I became a troop leader over at Camp Onofre. It is located off Basilone Road near the ITR (Infantry Training Regiment). This is where all the junior Marines or "boots" go to Infantry School. Boots are another word for fresh out of boot camp. As a troop leader I'd be in charge of a full barracks of Marines. There were four other troops leaders with me. We were all Vietnam Veterans too. These Marines we were in charge of were going to receive the best training. We'd be preparing them for their future in Vietnam.

Our days started before the sun came up. I'd wake up and smell the sweet scent of the beaches. We were just 5 miles outside of the Basilone Gate. This was the most southern entrance to Camp Pendleton. It bordered the city of San Clemente. The northern and main gate was near the city of Oceanside. It was beautiful out there. We'd start our PT runs that would go for miles. Sometimes in the sandy terrain, sometimes on the "hardball." That's another word for road or hard surface. Once the Marines showered, shit, shaved, and ate, it was off to the classroom.

We usually split the time from classroom and field. Sometimes you needed to teach in both. I liked it and was enjoying my time there. I rented a car one weekend and went to San Diego. I had a blast bar hopping and meeting girls from the local universities. I'd go and search for places that had "live music." It was just relaxing to sit back, have a cold beer, and watch these musicians jam into the night. What a blast. Other weekends I'd just go to the beach and have a great time. Every time I got in the water, it sent me back in time to the Cua Viet. I wouldn't see any of the California coastline. All I can see out of my eyes was the Cua Viet River. It's just the way it was. The more I stayed in Pendleton, the more I hung out at the beach. The more I thought of the NAM.

The training with the Marines was very realistic. The powers that be had constructed a real-life village that looked exactly like the ones we seen in NAM. A few bunkers were built and man it made me flashback. I'm not shitting you. SCARED THE HELL OUT OF ME. Once I crept over to the makeshift village, I had to peek inside. I did so with caution. All of a sudden, a thought raced through my mind: RUDY YOU DUMBASS, THE MARINES ARE BEHIND YOU WAITING FOR INSTRUCTIONS! I HAD TO THINK FAST. I leapt up from my crouched position and said "did you Marines see how I approached that bunker?" Instantly, in chorus they all responded "Aye Sergeant." I sold it perfectly. I went right into instructor mode. "Resto, Pittkins, Georgian, get up here and let's see you try it. Everybody else line up. You'll all get your turn." I watched them and stayed focused to see if they were doing things correctly.

I was starting to think of my Marine brothers in Vietnam. I could hear screaming and yelling in my head. All kinds of shit and emotions took me over. I let the Marines take five and excused myself to make a head call. I hauled ass to the trees and broke down in tears. They were floating like the Hoover Dam had busted open. I could hear voices in my head. Thoughts in my mind. They continuously bombarded me. Shit like" WHY'D YOU LIVE RUDY AND STEVE DIDN'T? WHAT THE HELL ARE YOU DOING IN THE STATES? SHOULDN'T YOU BE IN VIETNAM

FIGHTING? YOU JOINED THE MARINES TO BE A FUCKIN TEACHER? WHAT'S WRONG WITH YOU RUDY? YOU'RE WEAK MAN! WHY DON'T YOU KILL YOURSELF?"

I'm telling you I couldn't shut it off either. I just kept hearing these things repeat in my mind, all around me. I know that fuckin weasel (the devil) was trying to break me. His tactics are always the same and they were getting to me. I composed myself and ran back to the area where I was holding class. I could see the Marines taking this training seriously. I interrupted their training briefly with this comment: "Good job men, a word to the wise. Make sure you don't eat the chili mac in the chow hall. Otherwise you'll be in the head for an hour." Chuckles echoed the field. We went back to training and I stayed in my room the whole weekend. I kept having Vietnam invading my head, my thoughts, my everything. Sleeping became the hardest thing to do.

I had just released the Marines for the evening and headed to the chow hall. I sat down, had my meal, and excited the building. When I exited the chow hall, I heard someone say "RODOLFO IS THAT YOU?" That voice sounded REAAAAAALLY familiar. It couldn't be. NOOOOO. I turned around and sure enough. Who else could it be? Yup, that's right! None other than the infamous Manuel Orona himself. I couldn't believe it! What are the chances? I gave him a hug and asked him what he was doing there. He was finishing out his service at Camp Pendleton. He only had less than a year to go. We made plans to hang out and said our goodbyes. This was wild. From Pecos to Vietnam back to California. What are the chances? If Manuel was deployed to England, I'd miraculously end up with Embassy duty there. It was just so funny. I was glad he made it back safe.

I didn't tell anyone about the nightmares and thoughts I was having. I felt weak, embarrassed, and ashamed. I didn't want people to see right through me so I put up this wall. This wall to block out any and every bad emotion as best as I could. It never worked. I'd be walking in the store buying beer and a thought would flash in my head saying "WHY DIDN'T YOU SAVE US RUDY?" I'd run out of there leaving my beer and hide in my car. I would find out later on that I was suffering from heavy PTSD (Post Traumatic Stress Disorder). Also, something I later learned called "Survivor's Guilt."

I kept questioning myself saying "did I do everything I could that January 20th day? Could I have wasted a few more gooks and they'd be all retreating?" It really tore me up inside. That and the image of Steve laying there mortally wounded in that stretcher. I just kept telling myself I didn't belong here in the States. The weight of all that guilt and pain was immense. I had to do something about it.

Manuel and I started spending weekends together on our off time. We loved going down this street in East L.A. called "Whittier Blvd." There were always tons of girls, parties, and nice lowriders cruising. The dance halls would be crowded and lines to get in wrapped around the corner. I tried putting my mind at ease and resorting to fun. This was working and for a minute I thought I had this under control. I'd find out later how untrue that was.

I continued to my duties as troop leader. PT, map reading, calling in artillery, you name it. A lot of Marines came and went. I hoped that I had taught them enough to survive. Around

January of 1970, my Gunny Sgt Maddux called me into his office. I walked in and reported. "Stand easy Sergeant. Have a seat." I sat down and Gunny Maddux started to tell me they were releasing Marines one year early. Just the ones who went to Vietnam. Usually it was a four-year term. I was about to finish my 3rd year in the Marine Corps. He asked me if I was interested in leaving early.

I started thinking maybe my time was up. I'd done enough and was wiped out mentally. A change in civilian life might do my some good. The PTSD and horrific thoughts might go away if I'm not around this anymore. Plus, Trine and my parents had moved near San Jose in Northern California. It would be a fresh start and I could find work up there easily. Right then I decided I'd take the early out. My time in the Marine Corps was ending. I had no regrets but a ton of nightmares and pain. Maybe it'll go away I thought. How foolish that was.

I did the necessary paperwork and physical tests. In two weeks, I had two sea bags in tow. Off to Northern California as a civilian. A fresh start and family to be surrounded with. I caught the Greyhound bus and headed up the interstate. Taking in all the sights and scenery on my way. Seven hours and multiple stops later I heard my stop on the bus speaker. "SAN JOSE NEXT STOP." Time for me to go home. I stepped off the bus with uncertainty yet excitement. It was time to go career searching for Rudy Molina.

"All gave some, some gave ALL"

-Anonymous-

CHAPTER 20: UNCLE SAM's DISCIPLE

I had a positive attitude going into civilian life. My Dad hooked me up with a job at his company. He was working for a construction company as a truck driver. He was making decent money and it seemed fitting for me. No desk job, outdoors all the time, why not. I started driving dump trucks called "bottom dumps." My days started early and I was a "road warrior." Traveling all over different cities and towns in the Bay area. Some jobs were close and some were far. One thing I loved was coming home to an amazing Mother….and her home cooking.

The ebb and flow in my life had seemed to balance out. Sometimes you're high and sometimes you're at rock bottom. Uh, the game called "LIFE." My job made me feel I was doing something productive. I was saving money, had no worries, and being around family really helped. I had made the right decision. I knew all I had to do was close that chapter in my life. I was now in control of my life. I started to relax and become normal if you will.

I started dating some girls in the Bay area. On weekends, I would sometimes rent a motel in the city and hang out. I'd go to different restaurants, different nightclubs, or just walk the city. It was as if I was gaining my old life back. I started to smile more. Laugh more. Love more. I was really getting a hold of this. I'd show up at the yard early while the trucks were warming up. I'd shoot the shit with the other truck drivers. Someone always had something to talk about. The year of 1970 was finishing up. I had finished strong and better. I was excited for 1971. In

February of 71', that'd all change. The weasel came to fuck with me again. It all happened like this.

I was out in the city of San Jose. I was waiting for a load to be completed. The shipyard boss said his guys would be back from lunch in thirty minutes. I told him that was fine and I'd be back shortly. I was just going to cross the street to the hamburger stand for lunch. He gave me a thumbs up and I went for lunch. It was an unusually clear day for February. I was enjoying my hamburger and fries watching traffic flow by in both directions. An old Chevy truck with three Hispanic guys pulled in. As I turned away to continue watching the traffic, I heard a BOOOOOOOOOM!

I flipped the table over and dove for cover. I started reaching for my weapon but couldn't find it. I could hear the gooks laughing and the aroma of Vietnam set in. Oh shit, I'm back in the NAM? HOW THE FUCK DID THIS HAPPEN? I peeked around the table now flipped over and could see a banana clip of an AK-47. I'M FUCKED THEY HAVE ME NOW, THEY'VE COME BACK FOR ME. I YELLED "HELLLLLLLPPPPP, KLEPPEN, PERNA, BEESON, SOMEONE OPEN FIRE ON THESE FUCKIN DINKS!" When I looked up it was those three men in the Chevy. They asked me if I was ok in Spanish. I just stared at them. They looked confused. I took a look at myself. I had fries, ketchup, and Pepsi all drenched over me. Shit, I gotta leave. NOW.

I jumped up and ran away to the shipyard. I went looking for my dump truck so I could get the hell out of there. Thank God it was loaded. I hauled ass out of the yard and sped off. I passed the hamburger stand and saw the same three guys picking up the table I'd wrecked. Their truck had simply backfired. It sent me straight back to the NAM.

The guilt set it again. "RUDY YOU ABANDONED US! WHY'D YOU LEAVE US BACK HERE?" AHHHH FUCK, THIS IS HELL. I came home and went straight to the shower. My Mother knocked on the door. "Rodolfo, are you ok?" I replied yes and told her I had to use the bathroom. I said, "I'm going to shower now." I threw off my clothes, jumped, in the shower and turned it to FULL BLAST. When the noise and water of the shower hit my face, BUCKETS of tears followed the water down the drain.

I just couldn't shake it anymore. Over the course of two weeks, I had NASTY nightmares of the war. I was sleeping maybe 2 hours a night if I was lucky. Some nights I didn't sleep at all. I told my Mother I needed to sit down to talk with her. I wasn't going to tell her about my nightmares. Nor the hamburger stand incident.

I told her I was joining the United States Army. She leaned back against her chair and said "really?" She didn't knock me or talk down to me. She was stunned. I told her I was going to the recruiter station in San Jose the next day. I told my Dad to tell his boss I quit. I heard him say "But Rodolfo......." BAAAMM! I was out the door and off to see a girl I knew. The next morning, I got up early and showered.

I was going to get the hell out of here. Fast too. It was either that or I was going to eat a bullet. I just couldn't take it anymore. Once I was back in Vietnam, this shit would go away. I told myself that over and over. I waited at the U.S. Army recruiting station's door. Around 7:30 am, a Staff Sergeant was pulling forward. I could see his nametag. It said "FINKEL" and was attached on his upper right side of his sea green Army blouse. He walked up to me and said, "Can I help you Sir?" I replied, "I'm here to join on one contingency: I HAVE TO BE DEPLOYED TO VIETNAM OR DON'T BOTHER TALKING TO ME!" He smiled and said "step inside Misterrrrrrrrr?" I jumped in "I'm Rudy Molina nice to meet you." "Pleasure to meet you Rudy. My name is Staff Sergeant Finkel. United States Army." Within a week I was saying goodbyes to my family and friends...AGAIN. A two-year service I'd signed up for.

I landed back in Vietnam around August of 1971. It was in Da Nang airbase. The place where I felt happy the last time I flew away. At least there would be no more guilt. I would have a fresh new start in a new service: The Army. We went to our new base which was located right outside Da Nang. I was attached to the 1st Cavalry Division. The big patch with "the horse that never crossed." Yellow and black colored. I was transferred over to the 101st Airborne at Camp Eagle, Delta Co, 1/327. I became a squad leader.

The Army did things totally different than the Marines. In the Army, we'd all be flown in on helicopters to our location. Then we'd patrol for thirty days STRAIGHT. MAN, THIS WAS LONG. I was a squad leader and held the rank of Sergeant. We'd come back from the field after thirty days and go BUCK WILD. Three days of drinking, whoring, and bullshitting. We'd go to nearby Cam Ranh Bay and enjoy the beach there. The days passed by fast.

When we'd land into "hot LZ's" (landing zones under enemy fire), the helos wouldn't land. They'd stop 6-10 feet off the ground. You'd have to jump out fast or the door gunner would boot you out. It's that simple. Man, that was TOUGH to do. I'll tell you another thing that was hard: watching the helos disappear over the mountains. That was a LONELY feeling knowing we were on our own. The men I had under me showed great character and poise under any conditions. I was proud to be their squad leader. Up until that fateful November day. It was cloudy and raining hard. Foggy as hell. This day is right under January 20th 1968. Another catastrophic event unfolded. TRAGEDY struck once again.

It was a foggy November morning as we prepared to go on our next mission. November 28th,1971. Thanksgiving Day. We saddled up and waited on the tarmac for the helos to come. This time we would be going in CH-47 Chinooks. I remember it was raining too. It did surprise me that we didn't stand down till the weather broke. We didn't. We were given the green light to make our insertion that morning.

The Chinooks had tandem rotors and were a strong helicopter. They could yank a tank, deuce and a half, whatever, off the ground. Many times, they were used to salvage wreckages in rough terrain. Monsters. As I was squad leader, I made sure my men were loaded into the Chinook. When you lead, you're first on the ground and last to be loaded. As the last man was loaded, the door gunner stopped me. I asked him what he was doing! He told me the Chinook had no more space. "Get on the next one Sergeant."

I told him to fuck off and I was getting on this plane. I told him I'd sit on the helo floor. Still denied. These were my men and I NEEDED to be with them. I almost slapped the fuck out of him but he told me they were at capacity. "I CAN'T SERGEANT WE'RE FULL. "After haggling for what seemed a lifetime, I could see he wasn't budging. I finally agreed and stepped down from the ramp. I watched my men disappear into the rain clouds and fog. I couldn't wait for the next Chinook to hurry back to get me. About ten minutes later, all the helos and Chinooks came rushing towards the tarmac. Good I thought. Someone had some brains and ordered them to abort the mission. What I heard on the radio frequency is something that kills me to this day. I have never told anybody this and it hurts BAD even talking about. But the story must be told.

My Chinook with my ENTIRE SQUAD HAD CRASHED INTO A MOUNTAIN! I fell to my knees when I heard the Major come up and tell me the horrific news. NOOOOOOOOO IT COULDN'T BE! THOSE WERE MY MEN, MY BROTHERS IN ARMS. I SHOULD'VE BEEN THERE WITH THEM. I WENT FUCKIN BALLSITIC! HOW COULD THIS BE? I'M THEIR SQUAD LEADER! I SHOULD'VE DIED WITH THEM. I COULDN'T FEEL SHIT AFTER THAT. An angel was definitely watching over me. Once again, I'd cheated death. Once again, I'd rather have died that day with my men. The guilt came and whacked me off my feet like a tidal wave. I went COMPLETELY NUMB. I felt like the lowest piece of scum. Had that door gunner let me in, I'd have died with honor. With my men. I was instead riddled with guilt and shame. I'd failed MISERABLE.

There were hundreds of soldiers and crew on the tarmac. I couldn't see them. I couldn't feel them. The only thing I saw was myself; standing there alone. My head hung in pain. One hand was holding my rifle, the other holding fragments of what used to be my heart. Just like Steve and the 12 AmGrunts lost three years ago in My Loc, my men on that Chinook will NEVER be forgotten as long as I live.

There have been conflicting reports about the whole crash. 29 men and 5 crewmen perished in total. Some say they got hit by an enemy RPG, some say it was bad weather. The crash site had been wedged in rough terrain. The weather didn't help and halted rescue efforts. After a week, the crash site and corpses were recovered. I just felt NOTHING. My men were gone and it was a rainy, Thanksgiving Day. I have always hated Thanksgiving even today. It just brings back such a rush of emotions. I can still remember being out on the tarmac with my men. I can still hear their voices. I hope they met Steve and my Amtrac brothers in Heaven. I just hope. My men of 1/327 lost that day will be with me...FOREVER.

After that, I was basically the walking dead. I was given new men to be in charge of. We'd go on patrol for a whole month. Come back for three days, go back out. On one patrol, we were setting up and ambush near a trail. This was somewhere in the jungles of the Quang Tri province. (I Corps). Intel had been received that CHARLIE was using this particular trail as a supply lane. We set up claymore mines and waited. We didn't have to wait too long.

An hour later, seven gooks came diddy bopping along the trail. They wore Non-La's and carried AK-47's. They seemed pretty relaxed. VC type. We changed all that in a second. Once in the "kill zone" we blew the claymores. They were DECIMATED! We fired on them and they all were dead. At least we thought. I saw a gook get up and hobble away. I grabbed two soldiers and we went to hunt him down. All the while being careful. He might have had other "friends" lying in wait. We followed the blood trail and found him after ten minutes. We looked for his rifle and carefully crept up on him. I could see he had something in his hand. He looked at me as we laid prone on the ground. He was lying against a tree. It was a grenade in his hand. FUCK! We locked heavy eye contact. I sent an M-16 round right to his head. He died instantly.

We searched for his rifle and found it buried under some leaves. Once we got that, we were hauling ass back to the others. The men had buried the remaining six VC in a shallow grave. We exchanged information of our findings and called for an extraction. We were picked up and flown back to Camp Eagle. Soon we'd get news that the U.S. were starting to withdraw forces in Vietnam. We'd be among those first units. We were packing up and going home. Many soldiers in the unit were overjoyed. I didn't care to go back home early. For what? I knew what lied ahead for me.

"Life is like riding a bicycle. To keep your balance, you must keep moving"

-Albert Einstein-

CHAPTER 21: FIRST CLASS TICKET TO NOWHERE

I was on my way back to the world. We had a commercial airline taking us home. Some of the men and I were put in first class. Who gives a shit I thought! What do I have to look forward too? More hell and guilt. Ahhh man, I didn't care. I was on my way to Fort Hood, Texas to finish out my time in the Army. I didn't care and just wanted everything to be over with. Too much to take in.

Fort Hood is about 70 miles North of Austin in a small town named Killeen. That's the capital of Texas. Austin. I landed there and spent the next year or so playing Army. To be honest with you, I was still a zombie. The fact is I couldn't really tell you what we did there. Lots of field training, lots of PT, and each chance I got I took off the base. I found a few spots on the outskirts of town where I'd hang out. Nobody knew me there and I was perfectly fine with that.

The time blew by and I was out of the Army. I took a cab to the airport and bought a plane ticket. Destination: CALIFORNIA. I was going back to live with my parents. I landed in San Jose and took a cab to the house. Back to square one, back to more hell I thought. I just didn't want anybody to ask me about Vietnam. I never let anyone know I served in Vietnam. Sometimes I'd be walking through the grocery store with my Mother. All of a sudden, I'd see a man who would be looking at me. WHAT THE HELL IS HIS PROBLEM. His eyes told it all. He was a NAM VET. I COULD TELL. He had that "thousand-yard stare" as we called it. It was a look a Marine or Soldier had when he had seen too much death. It's like you'd look beyond and your eyes were much darker. After that I walked over the other aisle. I didn't want to relive it.

I started back at my old job driving a truck. My Dad's boss understood my reasons and hired me back. I was looking for something though with much more pay and BENEFITS. There were no benefits in truck driving. I started to look for jobs that would have that. Stability and security. I started looking for State and Federal jobs to apply at. Back then it was all paper, no online like today. I found a local federal agency and applied. After a month I had forgotten about it. One Friday afternoon, I was off work early. My Mother was cooking a huge meal. I sat outside reading the newspaper on the front porch.

My reading was interrupted by my Mother. I heard her yelling "RODOLFO, YOU HAVE A PHONE CALL." I laid the paper on my chair and went inside. "THIS IS RODOLFO" I said. It was the federal agency calling me. They said they had immediate job openings. The title for the job was correctional officer. Good pay and benefits. Security I thought. FINALLY. I made an appointment to go take some tests. After the tests were conducted, I did a physical and background check. I was hired. I had been assigned my first station. It was FCI PLEASANTON (now FCI DUBLIN). This stood for Federal Correctional Institution, Pleasanton.

I learned that federal inmates had been convicted for crimes in different states. Ones that crossed interstate lines or bigger cases. I was briefed about the type of inmates I'd be dealing with. MURDERERS, BANK ROBBERS, PIMPS, DRUG TRAFFICKERS, ARSONISTS, COUNTERFEITERS, you name it. I was given my uniforms and told when to report for work. Once I drove into FCI Pleasanton on my first day, I knew I'd be going into hell once again. Later in life, I'd get to see the other side.

Around this time, I started to date a Hispanic woman. We'll call her Martha. Martha and I were spending every weekend together. She moved in three months later. We moved to a house in the city of Milpitas. I was working at FCI PLEASANTON (25 miles east of Oakland) and we were living a good life. A comfortable night. I was praying to God that I could just have some normality. The nightmare and pain didn't stop. I wasn't going to tell Martha though. Yeah, she was my wife but I was trying to get over my pain. I didn't want her probing into my head. It's hard enough speaking about the NAM now. I just dealt with it the best I could.

"Marriage is the most natural state of man, and...the state in which you will find solid happiness"

-Benjamin Franklin-

CHAPTER 22: ALTAR BOUND

Life as a CO (Correctional Officer) was like being an inmate. The CO's had a rolling joke between us all. My Commander Rosell would always say "folks there's no difference between the inmates and us. We are all doing time. We just do it on the installment plan." I'll never forget that because it was true. When a convict gets sentenced to ten years, he does ten years STRAIGHT. A CO does his in increments of eight-hour days.

The basics of CO life are pretty routine. They were boring at times too. You took the convicts to and from chow, to medical, showers, etc. The numerous "head counts" took up a chunk of your day. If you were stuck to one housing unit, you stayed there your entire shift. It was like you were locked up too. The only thing that really changed in the institution was the calendar pages. Other than that, same routine different day. It became boring fast. I liked being outdoors and not enclosed the whole day. I told Martha I was going to look for another job. She supported my decision one hundred percent.

Martha and I had become very much in love. We were married by the courts in late 1972. We had a quick ceremony and went to dinner after. I was now a married man. We got along great and we never really had huge issues between us. The only issues were in my head. Sometimes we'd be walking in town and I'd hear a loud "POP" from the loading docks behind the stores. I'd almost shit in my pants and hold her hand tight. The sound made me hear the nasty "CRUMPING" sound that an artillery round released when impacting. Martha would look at me. She'd ask me if I was ok. I shrugged it off and told her I was just startled. I wouldn't let her know what I really heard through my ears.

Life was starting to carry forward in better ways than before. One problem started to drift into our relationship. I definitely wanted kids and so did Martha. Only thing was she wasn't able to have any. I was very upset when we found out this news. I tried to put that behind us. I enjoyed Martha and her love. She was very good to me. I wanted to have kids though. When I had the conversation with her, she was a woman till the end. She told me we'd have to divorce so I could find a woman to have kids with. She was sad but she had to let me go. I knew what she was saying was true. It had to end.

We drove to the courthouse a few weeks later and got a divorce. The judge granted us a divorce and commented how cordial we were towards each other. I told the judge there was no ill will between us. I just wanted to have a family. It was always my dream to have kids. Had Martha been able to, I'd never left her. Life takes you on twists and turns you'd never imagine. I hope Martha found happiness in her life. I moved back to my parents' house. Back to square one.

"A Father holds his daughter's hand for a short while, but he holds her heart forever"

-unknown-

CHAPTER 23: MY BUNDLES OF JOY

Work continued for me as usual. I felt like a toy robot each time I clocked in. The ones where you wind up the crank on the back and they just operate by themselves. I started to apply at other jobs that wouldn't require me being isolated. I just hated not seeing daylight for 8 hours. Watching convicts come up with ingenious inventions gave me a little laugh each day. Other than that, desk jockey for eight hours.

Around this time, I met a woman through a mutual friend. We'll call her Olivia. Olivia and I started dating about a year after my divorce. We'd go out to dinners, movies, etc. I asked her if she wanted kids and she was all for it. I had planned to get married to her once I heard that. We moved into a small apartment together. Life was going well. In October of 1977, I came home from work. Olivia had served me dinner and had a big smile on her face. She told me she was pregnant.

I was ecstatic and looked forward to being a Father. I had promised myself that I'd do my best to be the best Dad ever. Not like my Dad was with us. I was so happy I got on the phone and called my Mother. I called my sisters right after. Man, I was excited. Gisela was my first born, first daughter. I can't convey to you enough how happy I was. Olivia and I had two more daughters. Zenia is my middle daughter and Lynn is my baby. Each one of them are special and brought me joy I've never felt anywhere else. I finally felt happy inside and was glad I survived NAM to experience this life, this joy.

I felt my PTSD and Survivor's Guilt had been healed. What a fool to think that. I guess I was just happy it hadn't been bothering me. When I turned off the light, I'd just check on my daughters and smile. I had become someone worthy of these three little angels. I spend every second with them after work. It was a glorious time. We out to the parks and spent hours there. Everything we did, we did as a family; TOGETHER. Birthdays, holidays, family dinners, all done together.

I remember I bought the girls a huge trampoline and put it in the backyard. Man, I loved watching my three girls jump up and down. They got so good at it they started doing flips and landing perfect on their feet. I'd sit out there just enjoying my family. The best times of my life had to be with my daughters. No matter what, they'll always be Daddy's girls. Good or bad.

Around this time, my Dad did a miraculous 180. He quit drinking, abusing my Mother, and cheating on her. He became a "Reborn Christian" and turned his life around for the better. He was good to my kids and that's all I was concerned with. As far as our relationship, it was "acquaintance like" at best. The damage had been done there. I endured way too much shit as did my siblings and Mother.

We kept our distance and I was fine with that. One day we were all having a BBQ at our house. The whole family was there and we were having a fun time. My sister Trine turned on the radio. I heard her say "I love that song." I concentrated to listen what song was on. I didn't hear the song she was enjoyed. I was hearing some bitch on the radio. I could hear here clearly. It was Hanoi Hanna. OH SHIT!

"PTSD isn't a disease. It's a wound to the soul that never heals"

-Tom Glenn-

CHAPTER 24: HANOI HANNAH's NIGHTMARE

"Hanoi Hannah "was a bitch I'd like to forget. She was that communist loving whore that we'd hear on the Armed Forces radio back in Vietnam. Her job was all about mind-fuck troops operating in Vietnam. She'd interrupt our radio station and screw with us. To sum it all up, she was the gooks psychological warfare puppet. You would hear her voice while you tried to sleep in the field or back at base camp. Her real name was Trinh Thi Ngo. Every time we heard her, we'd toast to her and say "FUCK OFF TRAMP."

Her scripts were always written by the North Vietnamese Army. They also played a ton of songs that were anti-war. She'd make it a point to broadcast the fact that they were playing those songs in the United States. She'd also play recorded messages of Americans speaking out against the war. It was their theory that U.S. troops would listen to their own people rather than an enemy. They went against all of us. The U.S. Navy would be tormented too. Hanoi Hannah would name their unit and actual names of the crew members. Telling them they'd be hitting a mine in the water and all die a horrible death for nothing. Shit like that. Sadistic BITCH she was. She was treacherous. "How are you GI Joe, I see you lost a whole platoon yesterday in Khe Sanh. I told you death is coming for you."

She'd get on the radio and tell you by your unit that you were going to die." Drop your weapons GI, we will even let you live here with no repercussions." We'd make jokes about her and say" DROP YOUR WEAPON AND UNCLE HO WILL GIVE YOU YOUR WATER BUFFALO...AND RICE PADDY TO SHIT IN." There it is! Comical but she did get to you. When a certain unit was hit by the gooks, you'd hear her babbling on the radio. Laughing. Taunting. You name it. She'd call us by unit too. Her saying that we were next. "AMTRAC BATTALION, YOU'RE GOING TO BE SLAUGHTERED." That's how they played with you. Straight propaganda and head games.

I couldn't wig out her at the BBQ. I did my best to maintain my composure. I didn't want to freak out the kids or Olivia if I had a flashback. It was embarrassing and I still remembered the hamburger stand incident. So realistic, so dreaded. I excused myself and had my Dad watch the BBQ. I went to the restroom and looked in the mirror. Holy shit, I was watching a movie play right in front of me. I was running in the sand dunes of My Loc. All over again. Shit, SNAP OUT OF IT RUDY. Right then I heard a knock on the bathroom door. It was my wife Olivia. "Rudy you ok?" I replied "Yeah I'm fine Olivia, just washing my hands." I had escaped again. Thank God.

Hanoi Hannah really put her work in as a propaganda DJ. She would come on at least three times a day. The details and information she got were very accurate. Probably some American troop was banging here, who knows. It brought back my flashbacks though. If I saw her up front, I'd have put a round in her cranial cavity. Ironically, that bitch lived till she was 85. She finally met her demise three years ago.

"I have incredible motivation to go out and improve everyday"

-Alex Rodriguez-

CHAPTER 25: JOLLY GREEN GIANT

I finally got out of the CO job working with the Bureau of Prisons. I needed a change and got hired with the INS (Immigration and Naturalization Service). My first duty station was in the city of Fresno. Right in the middle of California. Central California. We moved and bought a house there. Olivia, the girls, and I settled in. I was looking forward to a new career. At least I wouldn't be chained to the desk. There seemed to be lots of opportunities in this agency. I wanted to climb the ladder fast. Sometimes in certain careers, getting relocated got you promoted much quicker. I put in requests for other duty stations after a few years. Around 1986, I got a chance to go to Presidio Texas. We moved and I started working there shortly after.

Presidio is a small town in western Texas. It stands on the Rio Grande river. This river is a major passageway for people crossing the border illegally. I think there's no more than 5,000 people that live there. At this particular job, I did a little bit more of everything. Identification checks, border crossing vehicles, semi-truck checks, you name it. The days usually flew by and much of the work details were outdoors. I was having fun. I was making a good living and the girls were growing at rapid speed.

Back in these times, the main thing we were looking for was drug and human smuggling. Especially in these small border crossings. As I stated earlier, a lot of illegal immigrants would take their chances crossing the Rio Grande. They usually would end up meeting their demise. Even if they were a natural born swimmer. Those currents were no joke and could take you away in seconds. It wasn't uncommon for a dead body to wash up to either side of the river. Just a typical day on the job. The INS was now called the Border Patrol. We'd wear these ugly green uniforms. I'm 6 feet tall and I looked funny in that uniform. Nobody liked the "greens."

Around this time, Olivia and I started having problems. She was becoming much more demanding about everything. I didn't have no vices either. I didn't smoke, drink, or do drugs of any kinds. Just the bitching and complaining kept up. It started to wear me down. My nightmares at night started occurring again. I started getting frustrated and grew tired of Presidio. Maybe a transfer would help us. A new start. I asked my boss Mr. Watson if there were any openings west of Texas. "I got an Inspector position in Douglas, Arizona. Put in for it, Rudy. Don't hurt to try." I followed his advice. Two weeks later, I was informed I got the position.

We packed our things and sold the house in Presidio. In a month we were gone. Douglas was a seven hour drive away. We made it there in one full day. We make some restroom stops and had lunch. Once we were there, I started unpacking. I reported to work the very next day. I received new uniforms and new schedules. I got a call from my Mother a few days later. She told me that her and my Dad wanted to move close to us. I told her it was a bigger town than Presidio and bordered the New Mexico line.

About a week later, I get a call from my Mother again. She told me they'd be moving over to Douglas. That was great news. I always wanted my kids to be close with their grandparents. From both sides. I loved it that my parents adored my daughters. They were constantly showered with love. Having them around would be a blessing. Olivia didn't think so. She started to keep my daughters away from my parents. I didn't like this at all. This fractured our relationship in a major way. Regardless of what others may think, this is the truth. It continued and continued with no resolution in sight. Another problem soon arose. MONEY.

Hell, I was working my ass off and pulling in overtime every chance I got. I'd come home dead tired and then have to hear her tyrant mouth. Its just the way it was. I started to seclude myself and go back to NAM. It just made me not want to be around anyone. I'd be walking with my girls but I'd be somewhere else in my mind. Finally, one night, Olivia came in the room. "Rudy you need to make more money. We ain't going nowhere here with this Border Patrol shit. Go get a higher paying job." I was making good money at the Border Patrol but with three kids and a wife to support, sometimes it would be stretching it. I started to do something I never thought I'd do. I started taking bribes. Cash bribes.

Life turned around for Olivia. Man, she was happy as could be with all the extra dough laying around. I still worked hard and still worked overtime. Problem was, the extra cash became a part of Olivia's life. We started to live a bit "higher" than the average. It started getting out of control. Olivia didn't care and loved this new pipeline of bread. I got tired of her playing games, not letting my parents see my kids, and her nonstop rants about money. I told her I was moving out and needed a separation. She flew off the lid. She was pissed off that I was going to leave her.

I said "separation" but I was mentally checked out already. Olivia knew I wouldn't be coming back. Her life of luxury was coming to an end. I didn't have a problem with that. "Rudy you think you're going to walk scott-free and leave? I'm going to make you pay." She did too. I didn't know what the problem was. We weren't getting along, she kept my kids away from my parents, and became greedy. She had no problem with her family being around my kids. This pissed me off big time. I knew things would be spinning out of control really quick. I was right on the money.

She knew things I was doing illegally. Cash bribes. For the protection of my family and others involved, I'll leave it at that. One thing I was NOT, was a drug smuggler and or ringleader. Nor did I EVER move any type of illegal narcotics on my person or my vehicle. THAT's the TRUTH. Olivia had been calling me threatening me and telling me I had to come back home or else. I was staying in my parents' house during this time. Olivia was playing more games and not letting me see the girls. She wouldn't drop off my kids to me.

Over the next week, things didn't seem on the up and up. One thing I noticed was a car tailing me for a few days. I could see cars behind me when I was on the highway and the streets. I tried to shrug it off but I just couldn't. I started doing stupid shit to see if I wasn't losing my mind. Stopping at greenlights, making sharp exits, illegal u-turns, you name it. I finally "made" an undercover when I swapped cars in a parking lot. I saw a man and woman in an undercover car. I'd never seen them before but I could see them looking in the direction I entered the lot. One swiftly turned around and looked to the corner. We locked eyes. She knew they were made. My mind starting going a 1000-miles a minute. Why am I being followed. This wasn't going to be pretty.

Three days later, I was on my way to my parents' house. I had just turned off the highway and headed South. Once I passed the second stoplight, I saw a line of undercover cop cars. What the hell was this? I saw the first car pop its lights on. I pulled over to the shoulder immediately. When I looked in my rearview mirror, there were six cars behind me. WHAT THE HELL IS GOING ON? They were all out of their cars taking cover behind their car doors. All had guns drawn on me. Nobody came up to the car. I heard someone on a bullhorn screaming "GET OUT OF THE CAR NOW." SHIT!

"WALK BACKWARDS NOW. KEEP ON COMING. KEEP ON COMING. STOP! ON YOUR KNEES NOW. NOW." I complied with all their demands. I had six to ten cops converge on me. I was placed in handcuffs immediately. Only one thing ran through my head. Olivia's words "Rudy you're going to pay for this." One cop flipped me to my side. "Rodolfo Molina, correct?" I replied back, "THAT'S THE NAME THEY GAVE ME!" That didn't go too well. "Ok smartass, you're being charged with conspiracy to transport cocaine. We'll see how funny that is when the judge sends you up shit creek with no boat or paddle. Hope you're a good swimmer. Anything else you want to say Mr. Molina?" I shot back quickly, "I WANT MY LAWYER." I was quickly read my Miranda Rights and thrown into the back of a squad car. Life as I knew it was over. The year was 1991. I was transported to FCI TUCSON. My freedom was OVER.

"Money will determine whether the accused goes to prison or walks out of the courtroom a free man"

-Johnnie Cochran-

CHAPTER 26: SNAGGED

"STAND ON THE YELLOW LINE. TAKE YOUR CLOTHES OFF, ALL OF EM' INCLUDING YOUR SOCKS. PUT EM' IN THE BAG. QUICKLY. LIFT YOUR LEFT FOOT UP. NOW YOUR RIGHT FOOT. RUN YOUR HANDS THROUGH YOUR HAIR. HURRY UP. OPEN YOUR MOUTH. LIFT UP YOUR TONGUE. PUT YOUR ARMS OUT. FLIP YOUR PALMS. LIFT YOUR NUTSACK. TURN AROUND. BEND OVER AND SPREAD EM'. COUGH HARD. GRAB YOUR ROLL AND GO TO CELL TWO. PIECE OF SHIT." BAAAAAAAAMMM! THE DOOR SHUT HARD WITH A LOUD CRAAAASSSSHHHH!

If you ever run into Johnny Law and he wins, that's your introduction into the world within. JAIL. LOCKUP. It's probably the most humiliating shit one can endure. It's meant to humiliate you. Anyone who has ever been busted will convey the same words to you. It's something I never thought I'd encounter but I did. Hell, ten years ago, I was working in one of these damn facilities. I hated it. Now I was an inmate/convict residing in one of those concrete jungles. On a "NO-BAIL" STATUS till I appeared in court. I knew I was good. I didn't do anything that could send me to prison. Not saying I was a saint. Just saying in the courts of the United States, it's law you are innocent till proven guilty. It's the other way around though in reality. I just wanted to plead my case and get back to the free world. I called my parents and let them know what had happened. They were shocked and I said not to worry.

The prosecutor in my case was relentless. I fought my case since a conspiracy carried a "life sentence." LIFE! "ALL DAY" was the word used in prison when you were sentenced to life. I couldn't believe this shit. I stayed incarcerated in FCI Tucson while my case was being tried. My lawyer said I had a great chance to only get a handful of years. I wasn't caught doing anything yet I HAD crossed the line. I wasn't mad about that. If I had to pay for it, I'd accepted that. But a potential life sentence didn't constitute my alleged crimes. Murderers were getting 8-12 years...for MURDER. My charges were nowhere in that ballpark. Around this time, President Bush and the U.S. had gone on an all out "WAR ON DRUGS." The sentences they were handing out on drug cases were astronomical! I kept a level head though.

The next time I was visited by my lawyer Mr. Kroychek, he had a devastating look on his face. This can't be good I thought. He had really been upbeat and said the case was looking good. They had no evidence, yada yada yada. It's like his confidence had been drained out of him in one shot. Then came those words out of his mouth. "Mr. Molina, I don't know how to tell you this in a nice way. You are screwed man. The sentence won't be light. I can assure you this. Prepare yourself for the worst. I'm terribly sorry Mr. Molina." He reached into his attache case and pulled out some papers. He slid it towards me on the table. It was about 20 pages attached together. I looked at the first page. I saw what I needed to see. It had that name "Olivia Molina's statement." BAAAAMMM! CHECKMATE RUDY, YOU'RE FUCKED! Those were my exact thoughts. Olivia had ratted me out. She'd done me dirty. In my mind, my life as I knew it was OVER! I sat back in the chair and looked up at the ceiling. WOOOWWW!

I told Mr. Kroychek there wasn't anything I had to say. I picked up those papers, shook his hand, and exited the attorney room. I was shackled from head to feet and escorted back to my cell. I walked into my cell I was sharing with an alleged embezzler. We'll call him Sam. He was a Hispanic man and very intelligent. He was charged with a few "white collar crimes." Big money case. I must've walked in defeated cause his words spoke my feelings. "Didn't go too well Rodolfo? Sorry to hear that man." I told Sam my soon to be ex wife ratted me out. He just sat on his bunk and said "that blows man." I learned later he got three years. I was happy for him.

A month later I was standing in front of the judge. The Honorable Judge Pearson. He read off my charges and asked if I had anything to say. I said I didn't. I was sacked and words wouldn't change a thing. Olivia's deposition she gave was the nail in the coffin. Judge Pearson handed down my sentence. "RODOLFO MOLINA JR, I HEREBY SENTENCE YOU TO 365 MONTHS. YOU SHALL NOW BE HANDED OVER TO THE BUREAU OF PRISONS. GOOD LUCK SIR." Yeah fuck you too I thought. I walked out of the courtroom NUMB. That's 30 YEARS, 5 MONTHS. GOODBYE RUDY!

At this time, my daughters ranged in ages from 9-13 years old. If I ever got out, they'd be grown women with families of their own. I had let them down as a Dad. I figured I was SCREWED. Olivia had betrayed me and I had the paperwork to prove it. Again, I have no problem doing the time for my crimes. Just the way it played out left a sour taste in my mouth. The time didn't fit the crime either. She'd done it for three reasons.

One is she knew I was leaving her ass for good. That was FACT. Two is she would have my girls all to herself. The last one was the kicker. She copped a deal with the government. They wouldn't seize the huge house I bought in California with illegal profits. All she had to do was flip on me. They squeezed her and didn't have to squeeze much. She kept the house and I got thirty years. Plain and simple. Anybody that doubts that, I'd be happy to show you my court transcripts. It might hurt some people to hear the truth but its FACT. On a side note, she still owns and LIVES in that house today. Go figure. By the way, YOUR WELCOME OLIVIA.

The ride back to the prison was uneventful. I heard the U.S. Marshals transporting me talking about the upcoming basketball game coming on that night. They were making plans to go to this new bar and grill restaurant in Tucson. Talking about having beers and hot wings. I tried blocking that shit out. I wouldn't be going out to ANY restaurant for a REAAAAALY LONG TIME. If ever again. Once I was escorted back to my cell I went to sleep immediately. I laid down thinking "THIRTY FUCKIN YEARS." In a week, a U.S. Marshals van came to transport inmates, me included. I watched every car pass us by on the highway. They were free and I wasn't. Next stop would be four days later. OAK PARK HEIGHTS SUPERMAX PRISON IN MINNESOTA. Goodbye world, Hello Prison Hell!

"Watch ye therefore; for ye know not when the master of the house cometh"

-Mark 13:35-

CHAPTER 27: BURIED ALIVE

After four days of a long bus ride and multiple stops, I finally landed in my final destination: OAK PARK HEIGHTS SUPERMAX PRISON in the state of Minnesota. What I imagined it being was not what I expected. For a "SUPERMAX" prison, I thought it'd be HUGE. It wasn't and had two sections of it. The first was for the "mainline or general population" inmates. These are inmates all housed together in different housing units of the prison. The buildings looked like something from the Bronx, New York. At least that was my outlook on it. The other half of the prison wasn't visible. It was basically underground in a nutshell. The Special Housing Unit or "SHU" as inmates called it. This was the place where inmates went to when they were high profile crimes. Another was fighting or caught with contraband. You'd be sent there as well.

Protective Custody or "PC's" housed inmates of a different class. They were considered "the dregs" or "garbage" of the prison system. PC was mostly filled with rapists, child molesters, or snitches. If they were housed in mainline units, they'd get a "bone crusher" (Christmas tree looking homemade shank) driven into their neck. They were despised. Formal law enforcement inmates were housed in PC too. I had a problem. I fell in that category.

I was a former CO for the Bureau of Prisons. I was working for the Border Patrol when I was arrested. I had to think quick. One inmate asked me while we were in processing "what are you here for? My response came quick, "DRUG TRAFFICKING." He looked surprised and it ended the conversation. I had to play that "role" or else I was fucked. I was hoping nobody found out about my past. I didn't want a "jacket" thrown on me as a "PC." Plus, they were slammed down all the time. They'd be let out one hour a day if that. Everyone was gunning for them too. Shortly after my arrival, I heard one inmate got "made." That's when they found out who you were and what your charges were. The next day he went sailing off the fifth tier. DOA. DEAD ON ARRIVAL. Welcome to prison. Federal Prison.

I was immediately sent to the SHU. It definitely was underground and the worst part of the prison. This part had a little twist on it. You NEVER came outside. If you got an hour out, it was in an empty room, like an empty concrete swimming pool. You had a small skyline window to see way up top. But you never got sunlight on your face. You never breathed fresh air. Never walked outside. Pretty much BURIED ALIVE. The CO's in there were shady bastards too. Smuggling in contrabands of all sorts and making bank doing it. The biggest thing to bring in was dope. Any kind and any amount. The price of it would be ridiculous in prison. These CO's were probably making more money doing that. They were treacherous individuals. I was walked into my cell. ALONE. Two doors caged me inside.

They didn't pair you up with a cellmate or "cellie" as it was called. That was someone who lived with you inside your cell. I lost all identity and was now inmate # 31810-008. This was meant to break you mentally. I made up my mind that I was going to be here for a long time. Perhaps the rest of my life. I did the best I could to shut out the free world as I knew it. Most of the people in the free world had already forgot about me. Besides my family and a few friends that wrote to me, that was it.

During this time, I got a "Pell Grant" and took up college courses. I wanted to use my time wisely while I was there. I became a bookworm and read anything I could get my hands on. I studied criminal law and majored in it. It made my days fly by as I was always in the law library. In just three short years, I earned an Associate's degree and a Bachelor Arts degree. In criminal law. Once I did this, I was transferred to another federal prison in Beaumont, Texas. I hadn't smelled the outside or seen daylight in THREE YEARS. Back in Texas. I worked out inside my cell religiously.

Over the next seven years, I maintained this mindset. I wrote to my daughters all the time but never received any responses. I figured Olivia took care of that and never gave them my letters. My brother Richard, sister Trine, my Mother, they wrote me all the time. For that, it is something I'm truly appreciative and grateful for. They kept me strong, kept me alive. Once my daughters had grown up, they started to write me. They asked to visit me and I accepted gladly.

It was great seeing my daughters. It had been seven years and they were all young adults. I couldn't believe how much time had elapsed and so many changes that occurred. It was great embracing them and hearing their life stories. They all had been brainwashed by Olivia but I pushed that aside. I just was happy to see them. Same for my sister Trine and my Mother when they visited me. I hated looking in their faces and seeing their pain. Pain I had caused. It made me feel worthless. I started to hate visits. I'll tell you why.

Visiting was both physically and mentally draining. To be honest, I dreaded it. When I'd get a visitor, I'd hear so much of the free world and it played with my mind. I'd hear stories of new restaurants that opened, trips to Disneyland, and new events unfolding. I'd also be able to eat food we didn't have available in the prison commissary. Hamburgers, burritos, hot food, sodas, etc. It played with your mind. I knew I wasn't going to those new restaurants for steak, I wasn't going to Disneyland, this place HAD NO DISNEYLAND HERE, and I had no control of what was happening in the free world. "The Outs" as inmates called it. When you're incarcerated, you just can't tell your family, kids, and friends to go pound sand. They're spending their own money and time to see you. I seen some men, GROWN MEN, crying like bitches on the phone. Begging their girlfriends, wives, family, to come see them. It mentally broke them. I figured when I first came to prison that I wouldn't concentrate on the outs. It made you weak. This was my world now. FEDERAL PRISON. If you're weak in prison, you'd become a lamb chop. REAL QUICK.

Over the years, prison life just came to be redundant and routine. Counts were eight times a day and the walls stayed the same color. The food was nasty in there and inmates would come up with new "menus" made out of items purchased in the prison commissary. Ramen soups were the most common form of "Cell food" in prison. They'd come up with all kinds of dishes with soups, cheese, chips, hot sauce, etc. We called them "spreads." They even made prison wine called "hootch" or "pruno." This was made with rotten fruit, lots of sugar, and yeast. It smelled and tasted like shit. It was a big thing in prison. Some inmates would make "prison oysters" and tamales out of store goods. Crazy things you see in there.

Things continued on in prison just as routinely as it was designed. I was having major flashbacks throughout my entire prison bid. Sometimes I'd be reading a book on my bunk or "cookie sheet" as inmates called it. A thin, metal layer wedged into the wall. It was super thin as was the prison mattress you were issued. I had many pictures in my cell but NEVER called it my "house." You'd hear inmates call their cells their houses. Man, I thought this ain't my house, lol.

Back to my reading, I'd get a smell of the Cua Viet. I heard people talking Vietnamese and I'd tremble. I'd look at the concrete wall inside my cell. It was like watching a replay of what happened on that fateful January 20th 1968 day. The smell was real and I'd see myself pinned down in the sand dunes. Holy shit, what is happening. I tried covering up my face but could still hear all hell breaking loose. The emotions would flood my mind and soul. I'd be sweating under my blanket profusely. Shit, this was hell. I'd be broken out of it by something like this: "COUNT TIME, LET ME SEE YOUR HEAD." I'd raise my head out and the CO on duty would look at me confused. He'd keep on stepping. Thank God. Over the years, it went like that. Sometimes, I'd dream I was on the Outs. I'd wake up and see a thick tan colored door. I wasn't free. I was in prison.

"ON YOUR FEET NOW. TURN AROUND AND CUFF UP. HURRY YOUR ASS, I AIN'T GOT ALL DAY." Typical start of the "turtles" flipping your cells looking for contraband. They were used for cell extractions too. This was when an inmate would refuse to cuff up or come out of his cell. They all dressed in all green uniforms and had so much protective gear on. Helmets included. They looked like the cartoon characters "The teenage mutant ninja turtles." They usually flipped cells just to make you uncomfortable. You'd end up spend the remainder of the day cleaning it up and being pissed off.

Inmates who refused to come out their cells would get a visit from the turtles. They'd all rush in with the first one holding a shield. The others would follow behind and rat pack the inmate. A smart and seasoned inmate would pour shampoo or baby oil in the front door of his cell. Hence the first CO with the shield would go down sliding and give the inmate an inch. Either way, in the end, they'd receive a royal stomping from the barrage of CO's. Pepper spray was their favorite tool to use too. The whole housing unit wreaked of it. It burnt your eyes too.

The nightmares and PTSD hit me like a machine gun going full blast. They became more painful and relentless attacks occurred. There was nowhere to run. I just had to deal with it and suffer. I kept thinking I was better off dead than being here in this hell. In prison, you either accept your time or go crazy. A lot of people cracked and would hang themselves with their bedsheets. I constantly thought of my fallen brothers. ALL OF THEM.

"Prison is like high school with knives"

-R. Butcher-

CHAPTER 28: TWO DIMES LATER

By this time, it was 2011. I'd been in prison most of my forties, all of my fifties, and now was in my SIXTIES. What a total WASTE OF TIME. I would still get visits, letters from my daughters and family, and make the occasional phone call. If there's one thing that hurt the most, it was seeing my visitors (whoever it may be at the time) leave. You'd watch them leave after saying goodbye and last hugs. Walking out to the free world, the Outs. I'd be walking back to my hell. A strip-search always awaited inmates when visiting was over. I never got used to that kind of shit.

A CO came knocking on my door the next morning. He spoke two words. "COUNSELOR MEETING." These were meetings you had with your prison counselor to see how things were going. He told me I had good behavior time accrued since I had no "writeups" for bad behavior. My release date would be early next year. 2012. I really never banked on it as prison officials always mess with your "gate date." That's the actual date you're released from prison. I will tell you I was very excited but smothered it. I didn't want to get my hopes up. The way I had my mind set, I was going to "max out." Meaning finish the whole thirty years. I wouldn't owe Johnny Law nothing after that. I let family know but told them it wasn't etched in stone.

The whole time I'd been wondering about all my Marine brothers I served with. I wondered how their lives where, married or not, kids, etc. I was hoping they all were doing much better than I was here. Locked in a cell with no key to get out. I always had it in the back of my mind of a "Scout Reunion." I was really hoping that would happen once I was released. I've always wanted to go to the Vietnam Wall in Washington, D.C. to honor my best friend Steve Sarossy. Sadly, I'd probably see another Marine brother on the Wall. Sergeant Ron Kovic. My squad leader in Cua Viet. The Marine brother I tried saving on January 20th 1968. I was 95% sure he didn't make it. He was in rough shape when Corporal Keaveney picked him up and carried him to safety. He'd been out there with me wounded twice for other 30 minutes. I'd give him my last respects too.

I called up my sister Trine and told her to search for Ron Kovic. I told her to research his name and see if he was on the Vietnam Wall. It was always a thought that never left my mind. By this time, I was serving my time at Taft Correctional Institution. This was about 125 miles south of Fresno. Out in the middle of nowhere as usual. I had been moved to the minimum facility called "The Camp. "We lived in dormitory settings there and the CO's were very relaxed. No fences and no locked doors. An imaginary line kept us from going "Out of Bounds." Prison term for being somewhere you shouldn't. I was now a short timer. My counselor confirmed to me a month later I'd be released next year. I didn't believe it. I put it in the back of my mind and waited to hear from Trine. When I finally did, I was FLOORED.

Trine sent me a letter saying that she had found out what happened to Sergeant Kovic. She said he was very much alive and he had written a book. The book had turned into a movie that won two Academy awards. He was awarded the Bronze Star with a combat "V." I couldn't have been any happier to know that he survived that day. He was paralyzed I know that. He couldn't move while I kept firing in the sand dunes. Once he was wounded the second and last time, he was done. The VA (Veterans Administration) doesn't sent out reports to you telling you what happened to your fellow comrades. It doesn't work that way.

I guess the movie had came out in 1989. I never watched much TV until I came to prison. In federal prison, there are no Rated "R" movies shown. So, I never got to watch it. I was really excited and proud of Ron. What an accomplishment. Good for him. I wanted to read his book immediately. I asked Trine if she could order me the book. Three weeks later, the book arrived in my dorm. I was so excited and opened it up immediately. I still have that copy today.

I read the whole book in a day and a half. To be honest with you, I was VERY disappointed with Kovic's book. I was upset that my squad leader hadn't written his book accurate. There were many details in there that didn't happen. Nobody left him behind abandoned. I stayed with him under heavy fire the entire time. Nobody abandoned us or ran away to the treeline. They ran out of ammo and went to seek cover too. The Marine who carried him to safety wasn't a black guy. It was Corporal John P Keaveney. A 6'2, 240 lb Irishman, who carried him out to safety. He's very much alive today. He wasn't killed in action. I took notes of the inaccuracies and wrote Kovic a letter. I made copies of that letter (which I still have today) and went to the prison post office. I mailed the letter to Kovic's home address (found by Trine) and attached a return receipt address form on it. Those are mailed back to you once someone signs for it. I hoped to hear back from Kovic. I never did. I did get the return slip back. SIGNED TOO.

This really struck me odd. I started to think maybe he "thought" that's what he saw. He was wounded twice and lost a lot of blood. Slipping in and out of consciousness and didn't really have his senses together. I DID. I WAS NOT WOUNDED. I WAS THERE. I had all of my senses. I just hoped he would've gotten back to me. It left me very upset. I hoped once I got out of prison, we could have a reunion. A Scouts reunion. I had served over two "dimes" in prison by now. A dime in prison means ten years.

"The secret to happiness is freedom….and the secret to freedom is courage"

-Thucydides-

CHAPTER 29: FREE AT LAST

The rest of the year went like any other prison year. The calendar changes but prison is basic. It just consists of routines, counts, and counts. Then more counts. No women, no fun, just killing time. My counselor called me in the spring of 2012. He sat down and explained to me a few things to look forward to. Adjusting and transitioning to life in the free world. I asked him why? He told me my release date was July 24th, 2012. I'd be going home. I'd be finally released from this hell. I couldn't believe it. Four short months to go.

It was a beautiful summer Tuesday in July. I didn't sleep the whole night. I was so excited like never before. Today would be the day I'd be released from prison. I wouldn't be inmate # 31810-008 anymore. I'd go back to my life as Rodolfo Molina. I gave all my things like TV, radio, store, away to other inmates to have. I wouldn't need them anymore. The date was July 24th, 2012. I was really happy and had paid my debt to society. I was now a free man.

Once I walked out of those prison gates, the air changed. It smelled sweeter and zero tension in the air. In prison, the tension is always in the air. You can feel it and definitely can feel when something bad is going to happen. I was overjoyed. I turned around, gave the prison the bird, and promised myself one thing: I'd never return to prison. I've kept that up to this day.

Trine and my oldest daughter Gisela were there to pick me up. I was happy and we all hugged. It was finally over. No more count time. No more lights out. No more visits under stupid ass guidelines, and no more strip searches. It was off to my parents' house in Modesto. A lot of family would be there to see me. I knew my Mother would have something cooking. She sure did. I hugged everybody and we ate at the table. Everything was going so fast.

Prison life is like a car going at 35 mph. Slow and boring. The highways were full of cars, people walking on the street, etc. In prison, men don't know what it's like to hear a bird chirping. We don't know what its like to hear a dog barking, a car horn blowing. All you hear is bells and the emergency horn when shit hits the fan on the yard. Riots, fights, stabbings, etc.

The CO in the gun tower on the loudspeaker shouting "YAAAARD RECALL." That tells inmates it's time to go back to their respective housing units. I only had two hours to relax with my family. I had to be at the halfway house to report in for my six-month stay there. It was located in the heart of San Francisco. In one of the shittiest areas known to mankind. The Tenderloin District.

"Never accept an excuse. Usually it comes attached with a failure"

-Adrian M Nunez-

CHAPTER 30: THE TENDERLOIN

Driving up to the halfway house was filled with mixed emotions. I wished that I had more time to spend with my family. It was back to another place now. Although I was in the free world, one slip up and Johnny Law would send me right back to the can. No ifs, ands, or buts. I had to play their game once again in order to maintain my freedom. I checked into the halfway house in San Francisco's "Tenderloin District." What a shit hole!

The Tenderloin District is filled with a high rate of crime. You name it, it happened there. A ton of drugs, drug users, pimps, hookers working the streets, etc. A bunch of homeless people littered the streets and begged for change. All I had was the $200 I got from the Bureau of Prisons. "Gate money" as they call it. Most people who are released from prison have a box of belongings and that $200 gate money. Having money in my pocket was like discovering women for the first time. I hadn't had cash in my pocket for a few decades. Cash in prison is considered contraband. If you're caught with it, its off to the SHU. No questions asked.

I entered the halfway house and talked to the guard inside. I had to fill out some paperwork and then I signed in. I was told the rules (I'll get to that) and handed a handbook. The guard then buzzed me in. "Molina, you'll be in Room 5." I headed upstairs and walked into Room 5. There was four to a room. Two sets of bunk beds were in each room. I saw the empty one on top and put my bag up. We had one dresser per individual and shared a small closet. The showers were a small "rain room" but had separating doors to them. A bit more privacy than I've seen the last 22 years. I unpacked and settled in. Around this time, my three other roommates introduced themselves to me. Marcos, a Hispanic, Paulie, an Italian, and Bryan, an older white guy. They were helpful and Paulie quickly shouted out. "Read that handbook Rudy. Its your lifeline." The other two nodded. I said, "Thanks Paulie, I'm going to do that right now.

The handbook was a list of rules and regulations. I'll try to remember the ones that stick out the most. First one was no drug use. Second no drinking alcohol. Third was no women on grounds. It also listed a ton of others. We had to sign in and out each time we left and came back. Drug tests were random and mandatory. You couldn't refuse this. The earliest hour you could leave the facility was 9am. The latest you could be back was 4pm. There was a count at 4:15 pm. SHIT, more counts. Oh well, got to play the man's game to be free...really free. When you left each day, you had to leave a detailed plan of your day. One slip up and they could "violate" you in a heartbeat. Violating means send you back to prison. There was a small dining hall that civilian workers cooked chow in. Food was great compared to prison food.

I started going to the Veterans center in San Francisco daily. I'd spend most of my days there until I had to walk back to the halfway house. I was going for treatment for my PTSD. I was also getting my paperwork done to file for my 100% disability. I knew I had to get that approved or I was screwed. Just think about it. I was now 65 years old. I had been in prison for 22 years on a cocaine conspiracy charge. A felon. Who the hell was going to hire me for work? I probably wouldn't even get a job doing stoop labor like a bracero. I had so many things to get accomplished. With only seven hours of free time, it really stalled a lot. I did what I could each day and pressed on. Whatever it took, I wasn't going back to prison.

I started taking these classes at the halfway house every night. They were mandated and you had to sit through this boring shit. It was common sense stuff but you know what they say." Common sense is like deodorant. The people that need it the most don't use it." I get it. I knew how to do things and get my life in gear. I had a plan and was doing my best to get there.

My kids used to come and pick me up. My sister Trine was usually there to visit. Gisela used to pick me up and she loved going to eat Thai food. Man, this food was so good and I loved it. We spent time talking after until I had to be returned to the halfway house. She'd explain how her cellphone worked and I was LOST. She's trying to tell me how to work things on her phone and I got anxiety trying to mess with it. It was like trying to teach Calculus to a damn Wino. I didn't know diddley squat about no cell phones or the other gadgets the world now utilized. I remember rotary phones and pay phones. 1991 sure was history. Phone books were obsolete. They didn't exist. The world grew in a mad rush. It doesn't wait for prisoners to catch up. Everyone's on play while prisoners are stuck on pause. Its just reality.

My little sister Velma lived around the area. She would pick me up and we'd go sightseeing, out to lunch, or just have coffee. I was always watching my back everywhere we went. Prison mentality I tell you. After a few times, Velma asked if she could bring a friend. I said, "why not?" One day I leave the halfway house and Velma is waiting near her car. Her friend is with her. Beautiful, light skinned, Hispanic woman. She introduced me to her friend. Her name was Beatriz. She was short but her eyes were filled with life. I was VERY interested in Beatriz.

Beatriz started to come and see me even without Velma. She'd come pick me up and we'd see each other. I told her I was going to the veteran center a lot for PTSD. Velma had filled her in on my history. Beatriz never cared about that shit. She just liked being around me and with me. Once while we were entering a restaurant, I grabbed Beatriz's hand. She opened it and grabbed mine tightly. A ton of admiration and excitement shot through my body. I hadn't touched or been with a woman in 22 years. I was liking this a lot. Soon my six months were up at the halfway house. Thank God! Now I'd be headed for house arrest for six months. I'd be doing this at my parents' house in Modesto. See ya Frisco.

"For to be free is not merely to cast off one's chains, but to live in a way that respects and enhances the freedom of others"

-Nelson Mandela-

CHAPTER 31: OUT OF BOUNDS

My Mother Genoveva had passed away in the time I was in the halfway house. I wish I had spent more time with her. At least she got to see me a free man. She passed in September of 2012. That woman broke her back for all of us. I'll never forget the kindness of her heart. Her sweet love and the way she made me feel: SPECIAL.

I had done everything by the book and it was off to Modesto. I would have to stay in my Dad's house for six months wearing an ankle bracelet. It only allowed me to go thirty yards or so. If I went beyond that, that damn bracelet would start to turn red. It would beep too. I'd get a phone call from the Parole dept. It would go something like this, "MOLINA, WHAT HAPPENED? YOU'RE OUT OF BOUNDS. GET BACK IN THE PERIMETER." I would have to explain to them I just went to check the mail. I'm supposedly free but still the constraints followed. A free man locked up in the outside world. Imagine that.

The ankle bracelet would never come off. You slept with it, ate with it, showered with it. I know how a dog feels when he's chained to the same fence for hours. That was me pretty much. My Parole Office (PO as we called them) was a condescending ASSHOLE. He'd love coming to my Dad's and check the house. Check the fridge for beer, see how many people lived there, check where I slept, etc. He LOVED his job you could tell. Piss tests were always conducted too. I always came back clean. NEGATIVE.

I had to occupy my time while these six months passed. I was going to have one year of Parole after this. I swear I can see why people fuck up and get violated. The system is designed to make you fail. Corrections is so big now. these companies are trading in the stock market. WALL STREET. Some include CCA, GEO, etc. Just to name a few. You don't believe me, look it up. Its facts. I couldn't wait to be free...REALLY FREE. To be able to go and live wherever I please.

I started looking up old friends and my search for the Scouts continued. I start to get myself comfortable with using a computer. Same thing with a cell phone. I messed with both every day. I began to send off my paperwork for my VA benefits. I stayed on this and pounded my mind with more knowledge daily. My Dad just relaxed around the house. We rarely talked. It was liking having a roommate you never knew before. Some things are just beyond repair. Our relationship was a prime example. My daughters would come visit me which was a blessing. They each had children now and were Mothers of their own. As I stated earlier, all grown up. I loved being a grandfather and embraced that role. I still do till this day.

The six months passed and I was released from the ankle bracelet. I was itching closer and closer to getting my ENTIRE FREEDOM back. No matter what they did, I wasn't going to fail. I had done enough of that. I was on the road to freedom. One thing that bothered me was Beatriz and I had become distant. She was working in San Jose and I was in Modesto. I didn't have a car and she didn't drive. DOUBLE WHAMMY. This was during my six months of house arrest. We talked to each other and I wanted to see her. When my house arrest was up, I got diverted. But I never forgot her touch. Her eyes full of life, full of purity.

I went to buy the newspaper at a local newsstand near my Dad's house. A woman was staring at me. I introduced myself to her. We'll call her Katie. She was a white lady and lived in Modesto. We started seeing each other and were quickly married a few months later. To be honest, she was simply a bedmate as I was to her. She ended up being a thief and her devious intentions came to light. I hadn't been with a woman for a long time.

She just filled the void. It was short lived and my heart was never in it. I filed for divorce two years later. Then I got a hold of Beatriz. I had a car now and was attending PTSD meetings at the Vet Center. We dated regularly and my heart was 100% hers. Beatriz was the one I wanted to be with. I told her I wouldn't let her go. That's another promise I've kept.

"Faith and prayer are the vitamins of the soul; man cannot live in health without them"

-Mahalia Jackson-

CHAPTER 32: DAMAGE CONTROL

After my one year of parole was completed, I was handed my release papers. I no longer belonged to the Bureau of Prisons. I was free to do what I pleased. If I wanted to move to Ireland, I could do that. It was such a relief. The year was summer of 2014. I was establishing myself little by little. I had my driver's license, bought a new truck, and received my VA benefits. I could live comfortably without the struggles of finding a job. It was FINALLY OVER.

My Dad passed away in November of 2014. To be honest, I had mixed feelings about it. I can tell you I wasn't crushed over it the way I had been when my Mother passed. It was just never there and our relationship was more like an "acquaintance" type. After that, Beatriz and I moved in together. We bought a house in Coulterville, California. About 30 miles West of Yosemite National Park. I was living the best I had ever lived. We got along great and each day was filled with love. Filled with an abundance of laughter. Filled with peace.

I started making more time for my daughters and would visit them frequently. My ex-wife Olivia still created problems in my relationship with my girls. I tried to brush it off and continued to do my best. I hadn't been there in their lives for 22 years. There's no possible way you can truly make up for that. I get that and take full responsibility for that. There's also a point when how much is enough. Often, people stay stuck in the past. When this occurs, life keeps on passing you by. I wanted to be in my daughters' lives and re-establish a healthy conduit between us. I just don't want to be crucified forever for my wrongdoings.

I continue to press on and do what I can to rebuild, to start fresh. Love is a two-way street though. You get what you give. I remember a friend saying, "One-way love is no love at all." That is so true.

I met a nice Marine veteran named Duke Cooper. He is the CEO of AMERICAN VETERANS FIRST. A non-profit organization established to help veterans in any kind of way possible. They do wonderful things there and it's like a second home for me. For many veterans, it's the only place where they find comfort. I tell you, it was Duke Cooper who kept encouraging me to write my story. I was a bit on the fence at first. I finally agreed and kept coming back to AMERICAN VETERANS FIRST in Modesto. I never stopped and now I am a proud Board member. I am so lucky to have Duke supporting me through my hard times. In September 2016, I heard Ron Kovic was having a book signing at a Manhattan Beach bookstore. I was THRILLED. I invited my childhood friend Lupita Ramirez and her boyfriend to come with me. They gladly accepted and I took my copy of Kovic's book to be signed. The original copy my sister Trine had sent me in prison.

We arrived at the bookstore and walked in. About thirty people were in line to have their books signed by Kovic. I could see him smiling as he signed each book. He was in a motorized wheelchair now and looked happy. When I finally got up for him to sign my book, he shook my hand and signed my copy. I surprised him and said, "DO YOU REMEMBER ME?" He quickly recognized me after a few seconds. He replied "Nice to finally see you again Mr. Molina." I brought pictures of us in Vietnam together. He was overjoyed and apologized for not getting back to me.

Lupita had recorded our entire conversation which lasted about 12 minutes. I gave him my number and he promised that we'd get together soon. He introduced me to his girlfriend Terri Ann Ferren. She was a very nice woman and thanked me for saving his life. He told the people around him that I was the one who bandaged both his two wounds. People in line were shocked. I didn't want to take up his entire time so we made plans to meet up in the future. I wished him well and we left. It was 48 years that I hadn't seen Kovic. I was happy he was alive and making the best life had to offer him.

In the ensuing months, we exchanged a few calls and e-mails. Then in the summer of 2017, I never heard back from Kovic again. I wanted to tell him the good news about finding four scouts. I had got a hold of Kleppen while I was finishing my prison term in Taft. I located Farmer next. He lives in Florida. Perna was located next. He lives in Southern California. Rhodes lives in North Carolina. Kleppen lives in Florida. Finally, Kovic was located but now I've lost all contact with him. All the Scouts want to have a reunion with our squad leader Kovic. I'm hoping he'll read my book and get in contact with me or any of us. Anyone who can help in my search, it'd be much appreciated.

"Be happy for this moment. This moment is your life"

-Omar Khayyam-

CHAPTER 33: OAK RIDGE HORIZONS

Beatriz and I are happily married now. We continue to live in the small, mining town of Coulterville. The population here is 115 people. We don't even have a street light in our town. Our house is perched up on the top of the mountain. We have each day to enjoy God's beauty way up here. Secluded from the roving sounds of motorists on a busy highway. The only noise you hear are the many kinds of wildlife that we share our land with. The animals we have are quite a few. I swear, if you looked at our yard, you'd think we'd robbed Noah's Ark. Turkeys, dogs, birds, goats, chickens, you name it.

Sometimes I'll wake up early in the morning and go feed the animals. I'll scare off a few coyotes who are protected by the fences and my dogs. They still creep up and try to get one of my chickens. It reminds me so much of Vietnam. Sappers coming up to the wire trying to sneak in and kill us all. I tell you, the visions never leave me. The NAM. Steve and the twelve other heroes will always be with me. The same goes for my platoon that went down in that Chinook Thanksgiving Day of 1971.

Sometimes I'll sit in my yard and just watch the sun come up. I can see the beauty and feel the tranquility of this peaceful life. Being here with Beatriz is a blessing itself. I can truly say throughout my life, I've had an angel watching over me. I've been blessed with all this time on earth. Good or bad, I've tried to make the best of each day: EVEN IN PRISON. My wife and I have made our decision to leave the country for good. Here's why.

I will always be treated as a second-class citizen here in the United States. I've paid for my crimes and never have complained about that. I have done the appropriate actions to be released and finished all the necessary paperwork. The thing that gets me is when I'm pulled over. All a cop has to do is punch in my name: WAHHLLAAA! WE GOT A FELON HERE. I can't even vote. I can't even own a gun. Hell, I can't even be around people that have guns on them. If I do, it's off to prison. END OF STORY!

Last year, I traveled to Mexico to visit an old friend of mine. When I came back to cross the border at the San Ysidro/Tijuana gate, man they tore me up. I was whisked out of my car and taken to a holding cell. I had to empty my pockets and take off my shoes. Then they did a search of my person. They moved a metal detecting wand around me to see if I had any knives or guns. I'm sure they had a few drug sniffing dogs go through my car. I wouldn't know. I was in a windowless holding cell. FOR A WHOLE HOUR. They finally came back and threw me my keys. One Border Patrol agent said, "YOU'RE FREE TO LEAVE." He immediately walked out. Its shit like this that I refuse to endure for the rest of my life.

I've done my time and paid my dues. This shouldn't "blackball" anyone forever. WE ALL MAKE MISTAKES! Some get caught and some don't. The point is WE ALL SCREW UP. That's the problem with people. They all want to be "right finders." When the finger gets pointed at them, they fold up like a piece of paper. PERIOD. I fought for this country twice under two Armed Services. That should account for something. In today's world, it doesn't.

When we leave and start a fresh life in Mexico, its going to be amazing. I will no longer be classified as a FELON. I will not shit a brick if a Mexican police man pulls me over. I will not have to worry about getting yanked out of my car. Thrown to the ground like some dirtbag. Subjected to searches and drug sniffing dogs jumping inside my car. I'll just be "Rudy" over there. That's the way I like it. Beatriz and I will stay with her family till we find our own place. We plan to build our own house. Nobody will be able to bother me nor harass me anymore. That gets old quick. As I stated at the beginning of my story, I got at least a solid ten years left before I turn into Mr. Magoo. I want to make everyday count and trust me, NOTHING will get in the way of that.

As I'm sitting here writing my story, I feel the warmth of the fire burning. Beatriz is cooking up a storm and the aroma has saturated the house. She occasionally will look my way from the kitchen. Her eyes tell me a thousand times "I love you Rodolfo." She doesn't have to say it. This is the first woman I can honestly say wants nothing from me except my love. Not money, not fame, not a free ride, JUST MY LOVE. I feel it. I know it. I believe its avocado chicken tonight. Man, she can cook. I just reloaded the fire with four more logs. The fire was dying out so I had to bring it back to life. These logs will last us all night. It's the same way with life in general. When you are down and out, you have to pick yourself up. When you come up, you have to come up STRONGER. Ignite your soul with a vengeance! Never let that flame go out. Once it does, GAME OVER. This is the reality most individuals have trouble dealing with. They have no flame left. I never knew life could be this great. The BEST I've ever had.

The fire is now hotter than ever...my soul feels the same way today. I FEEL REJUVENATED! Blessed by God. I never imagined it would be this amazing. NEVER QUIT in life and never let doubt seep into your soul. It'll destroy you faster than a balloon loses its air. Failing is ok, we ALL fail. Yes, we ALLLLLLL FAIL. Only those individuals who get up will cross the finish line. The rest will make excuses. Losers will always tell you why their dreams never came true. But a WINNER, A CHAMPION, they will tell you HOW they made their dreams become a REALITY. I'd love to keep on writing but Beatriz just called me over to the table. Dinner's ready. If you want to know what makes my life amazing, its moments like this right now. I get to live HAPPY each and every day. THERE IT IS!

BONUS CHAPTER: CALLING ALL BATTALION SCOUTS

I recently have been in contact with all the remaining Battalion Scouts that are still alive today. I have not been able to locate Lance Corporal Evans. He is the last one to be found. From the very day I stepped out of federal custody in 2012, it has been my goal to have a reunion. A Battalion Scouts reunion. We were an elite unit consisting of ten Marines. Highly trained and lead by our squad leader Sergeant Ron Kovic. Here is an update on the Battalion Scouts I have found. Two are missing.

-Chuck Rhodes resides in North Carolina.

-Dennis Kleppen resides in Florida. He retired from the Marine Corps as a MASTER GUNNERY SERGEANT.

-Ron Farmer resides in Florida.

-Gene Perna resides in Southern California.

-Ron Kovic resides in Southern California (not sure if he still does). Lost contact 2017.

-L.Cpl Evans still has not been found.

In 2017, I traveled to Vietnam along with Lt. Richie Reynolds' brother Kevin. I had a plaque made for Steve Sarossy. I placed the plaque on a tree near the actual site he was killed in action. It was signed by over 100 people. Duke Cooper signed it first. I also traveled to the Vietnam Memorial Wall to honor Steve Sarossy. I went there with Steven Loya. It was a great experience and I have continued to heal since then. I am now 71 years old. I believe the remaining Battalion Scouts are around my age.

Again, my goal is to have a reunion. I have been in contact with each of these scouts listed above. I have lost contact with Ron Kovic. I don't know if he moved or changed his phone number. We'd all love to locate Kovic and Evans. Any help in this matter would be greatly appreciated. You can reach me at rudymolinajr@gmail.com. Thank you for reading my story. I was blessed to have served and fought with these fine Marines in Vietnam. God Bless you all and SEMPER FI.

ACKNOWLEDGEMENTS

There are so many people I have to give thanks to. I would like to start off by saying thank you to all who donated on my Go Fund Me page. Without your generosity, this book would've never left the ground. Forever I'm thankful for you all:

-Dennis Williams

-Richard Molina

-San Juana Orozco

-Beatriz Molina

-Steve Fry

-Velma Garcia

-Steve and Kathy Holmes

-Keith Lewis

-Jesus Teran

-Thomas Sobiieski

-Vicky Lattone

-Trine Lozano

-Robert Jordan

-Irma Camarena

-Sara Reyes

-Gene Perna

-Jim Peiffer

-Gisela Ruiz

-John Keaveney

-Charles Rhodes

-Steve Loya

-Joe Lattone

-Bruce Goins

-Jerry Lynch

-William B McKinney

I want to thank my wife Beatriz Molina who has always been supportive. She kept inspiring me to write my book. Whether good or bad, she has always been encouraging me to continue this hard journey to get this book out.

To my three daughters. Gisela, Zenia, and Lynn have each in their own way been a major part of this book. Whether they know it or not, they have helped me put this book together in the way it was told. My love for you three will never stop no matter what you may think of me. You can either accept what is written or continue to be in denial of what I have witnessed, lived, or experienced the last 30 years.

To my good friend Jesus Teran who worked with me as an Immigration Inspector in Douglas, AZ. Thanks for believing in me during the good times and the bad. Jesus you are a true friend indeed.

Thank you to my sister Trine Lozano. You never left my side regardless of the situation. You have always been there for me and I am grateful to have a sister like you.

Another true friend to thank is Steven Loya. Steve, you've been there for me all the time. If I need to talk with someone, You're the person I call. Your encouraging thoughts conveyed to me on my bad days have always been appreciated. Thanks Steve.

Duke Cooper, the CEO of American Veterans First, was the first Veteran who heard my story told at the Vet Center in Modesto. It was October 2016. When he heard my story, he approached me and told me we needed to talk. Since then, Duke has been instrumental in getting the word out of my story. He also encouraged me to write my story and experiences about Vietnam and Ron Kovic. To this day, he's given me tons of encouragement. Duke is the type of guy that looks beyond your past (as in my case) and only sees the person you are today. I thank Duke for his honesty and friendship.

Jim Nunez, another true friend, and Vietnam Veteran. Also a Silver Star recipient. You've been an inspiration to me in the short time I've known you. Our stories have many similarities that it scares me when I look at the whole picture. I truly do believe that a higher power put us in the same path. A path in order for this book to be written by none other than his son, Adrian Nunez. He is also a Marine Veteran and brother in arms. Adrian and Jim, thanks a million.

ECHOES OF AN ANGEL

My name is Gisela Ruiz. I'm the oldest daughter of Rudy Molina. To me, he's my Daddy. My SUPERMAN. He still is today. Life growing up with my Dad was truly amazing. He brought so much joy to my sisters and I. I know in my heart he did his very best to make us happy. In 1991, my world as I knew it came crashing down. All in one shot. ABSOLUTELY DEVASTATING!

My Dad was arrested and convicted of conspiracy to transport cocaine. We found out at a family outing through my Aunt Trine. She is my FAVORITE Aunt. I can never thank her for all she did for us girls while my Dad was incarcerated. He was sentenced to THIRTY YEARS in Federal Prison. When I heard thirty years, it rocked me to the floor. I felt the same way when you pull the plug out of the television. The sounds of energy, excitement, and life disappeared as I knew it. With my mother working, I took on the role of a mother. Watching my two younger sisters became a priority. I was never the same. My love for my Dad NEVER once buckled. I knew he loved us. He showed it and lived it. To be honest, I grew stronger.

The holidays became just another calendar day to me. Those days used to be the best. Now I had come to hate them. Birthdays, no big deal. Thanksgiving, no comment. Christmas, the worst of them all. They didn't have the same feeling anymore. They meant nothing. It only brought a ton of emptiness. I never blamed my Dad for anything. He was just trying to give us his best and he made a huge mistake. It sucks when you have to sit there and watch individuals having a great time. Knowing how you used to be happy like them. Now all you have is a handful of crumbs if that. Nothing but sadness and depression filled my heart. Memories replayed in my mind constantly.

I recall my Dad buying us a huge trampoline. It was like he bought us the best thing ever. I'd get on the roof and leap off straight to the trampoline. All the while making sure my parents didn't catch me. These are some of the fondest memories I have. One of my favorites at the very least. My Dad would come out and watch us in awe. He was a "hands on" Dad. Always watching over us.

My Aunt Trine kept the communication line open when my Dad went to jail. I was 11-12 years old. If we wanted to visit him, it was up to us to find our own way. Harsh but it is the truth. At night, I'd think of my Dad and rewind the fun times in my head. I'd tell him I love him. I was hoping he could hear that from me, even if he just heard my echo. My fear was those prison walls would cut off that love. It never did. As we grew up, we'd go see my Dad in prison. We'd be so happy to see him but sad at the same time. It reminded me what I missed so dearly. Every time the visits were up, we'd hug tight and say our goodbyes. He'd be standing there waving until he disappeared back into that door of hell. PRISON.

You get used to the long lines, the searches, and walking into those gates. With that comes the 15-minute phone calls and the letters from Dad stamped "FEDERAL PRISON." My love for my Dad never changed one bit. I went to visit him and accepted every phone call he made to me. For state prisoners, you stay incarcerated in your respective state. For federal prisoners, you can be incarcerated ANYWHERE within the United States. My Dad was housed in Minnesota, Texas, Arizona, and even Pennsylvania. His last housing unit was in Central California. Close to us.

After 22 years, my Dad finally walked out of prison for good. My Aunt Trine and I were there. I'd waited for this moment for 22 LONG YEARS. Although, he'd be going to a halfway house it didn't matter. We were going to make the best of it. We did too. No more phone calls that were limited to a measly 15 minutes. Interrupted every 3 minutes by that annoying voice, "YOU ARE ON A PHONE CALL FROM AN INMATE IN A CORRECTIONAL FACILITY." As if I'd thought he'd been at Disneyland the last 22 years. Lol. No more eating vending machine food with CO's watching every move, every minute.

My Dad's halfway house was located in San Francisco. Every Saturday, he'd have four hours of freedom. My sisters and I took every opportunity to see him. I didn't care if it was my last dollar or bill money. I'd work around that. I wasn't about to miss anymore time with him. It was OUR time now. Eating Thai food at the local mall was our favorite. The good times were being relived and a new path was in the future.

The thing I wanted most for my Dad is to be happy. Since he has been with his current wife Beatriz, I know he is in good hands. She is a loving woman who has made me feel good since meeting her. She has a glimmer in her eyes, full of love and life. She has welcomed me with open arms and damn, she is a GREAT cook. I know my Dad is where he needs to be in life now.

I want that to continue to his very last day. I support him in any way I can. Just like he's done for us.

Don't get me wrong, I went through my own tough times. Drugs, partying, drinking, etc. I just wanted my hero, my Daddy back. Everyone has their own vice. We often self-indulge a bit too much at times. It is that very thought that sticks to me the most. We shouldn't be so judgmental of others. We all have screwed up. We never had to start "fresh" since we always have had a strong bond. Everyday is exciting. We talk every day. My Dad has always been there for us even through the hard times.

If there's one thing I could say to my Dad it'd be this: Thank you for being you. Thank you for being the most AMAZING DAD any daughter could ask for. "LOVE" is the perfect word to describe my DADDY. My HERO. He'll always be my SUPERMAN. He just doesn't wear a cape. Lol.

ABOUT THE AUTHOR

Adrian M Nunez currently resides with his wife in Las Vegas, Nevada. They live peacefully near the famous Las Vegas Strip. Adrian served in both the United States Army and United States Marine Corps. He is also the author of WOUNDED: Based on a True Story.

Rudy and his Wife Beatriz today.

Made in the USA
Columbia, SC
13 March 2019